Word Processi
with WordPerfect

Book 1: Elementary

Also by Jenny England and Wendy Glew in this Series:

Word Processing with WordPerfect
Book 2: Intermediate

Word Processing with WordPerfect
Book 3: Advanced

An Activity Print-out File containing worked 'answers' is published to accompany each title.

Word Processing with WordPerfect

Book 1: Elementary

Jenny England
Wendy Glew

Stanley Thornes (Publishers) Ltd

First published in 1993 by:

Stanley Thornes (Publishers) Ltd
Ellenborough House
Wellington Street
CHELTENHAM
GL50 1YD
UK

A catalogue record for this book is available from the British Library.

ISBN 0 7487 1695 5

'Qwerty' drawings by Eric Goodchild
Typeset by Paul Manning
Printed and bound in Great Britain at The Bath Press, Avon.

The authors and publishers would like to thank the RSA for giving their permission to include the Word Processing Stage I syllabus and past exam papers.

Contents

v

Unit 9: Adjusting Line Length

Section 2: Supplementary Activities

Section 3: The RSA Stage I Word Processing Syllabus

Section 4: Exam Practice

Section 5: WordPerfect 5.1 Instructions

Index

Introduction

> Hello, I'm QWERTY. I'm here to help you with my handy hints and advice. If you've never used a self-study book before, don't worry, the instructions are easy to follow and, if you are in a class, help is always there if you need it!

Do you want to learn word processing skills?

Would you like to achieve an elementary qualification?

This book is suitable for you if you have already achieved your RSA Stage I Typewriting Skills qualification or have good keyboarding skills and now feel ready to progress to word processing.

Whether you are using a word processor or a computer with a word processing package, think of it as a sophisticated typewriter and do not be afraid of the equipment. Word processing simply means the processing of text so that you can amend your work quickly and easily without the need to retype. This is obviously a benefit to both you and an employer.

The equipment you will be using is known as 'hardware' and computer programs (like the word processing package you will be using) are known as 'software'. Computer programs are simply instructions, stored on disk, which tell the hardware how to behave. As you will be storing your work on disks, always handle your disks carefully.

How to use this book

Whatever your reason for working through this book, you will obtain the maximum benefit if you read the instructions and work carefully through all the Activities which follow. You will find that the Activities have been designed just for you, so that you can work on your own at home or in a class situation, in which case ask your tutor or training supervisor for help whenever necessary.

Although you will be working mostly on your own, you will find that learning is much more meaningful and enjoyable when you work at your own pace and, of course, you will develop some very useful personal and employable skills.

By working through this book you will learn all the basic word processing functions for your system so that you will be able to produce simple business documents, such as letters, memos and tables, to a high standard. You will then be ready for the RSA Stage I Word Processing exam and once you have achieved success at this level you may decide to work through the intermediate packages leading to the RSA Stage II qualification.

Proof-reading

As you complete each Activity in this book you must check your work carefully before you print out — this is known as proof-reading. With practice you will find that the accuracy of your work improves but you must still proof-read and correct the screen copy of each completed Activity. In order to gain the maximum benefit from this book and develop your proof-reading skills to exam level, the authors strongly recommend that you check each Activity, on completion, with the worked examples in the accompanying book, *Activity Print-out File.*

Presentation

By working through the Activities you will learn how to present your work attractively and correctly. Whether you are at work, applying for a post, or sitting an exam, presentation of your work is important as it represents your own personal standard.

Production

You will find timed Production Activities throughout this book and specimen exam papers to help you develop your word processing skills to an employable level and achieve success in your exam. You should complete the Activities in approximately 10-12 weeks, allowing for 2 hours per training session. You will then have time to complete practice exam papers if you intend to sit an exam.

There is also a Supplementary Activities Section in case you need extra practice. Only complete the Activities in this Section if you have the time.

Note: Core Text Processing students should complete Units 1 and 2 only before beginning work on exam papers. CLAIT students working to the word processing assignments should complete Units 1, 2, 4 and 5 only before beginning on the assessed assignments.

Section 1:
Instructions and General Activities

1 Editing Text

Read the instructions below first and then follow them to complete Activity 1.

Getting started
If you have not used WordPerfect before, and you are working on your own, you may need to consult your machine manual to help you get started. You will need a formatted blank disk on which to save your work.

Switching on/loading WordPerfect
1 Check equipment and switch on
2 Load operating system
3 Insert work disk into floppy disk drive
3 Load WordPerfect (this automatically creates a document)

NB Machine set-ups vary — consult your tutor/supervisor or machine manual if necessary.

Status line
When you have selected WordPerfect your screen will appear blank except for a flashing light which is known as the CURSOR and the STATUS LINE at the bottom right which should show:

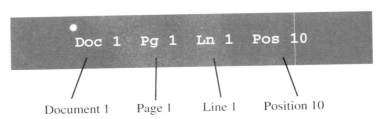

The status line shows you the current position of your cursor, so it will change as you key in your document. The default (normal setting) for WordPerfect gives you left and right margins of 25 mm (1 in), which is shown by the position in the status line. Printing is set at 10 pitch (10 characters per inch).

Drop-down menus
Drop-down menus are also available in WordPerfect. To use these menus, press **ALT** (menu bar appears), select option required (pull-down menu appears), and choose the function you want. To exit, press **F7**. These menus can be used instead of/in addition to normal function keys, but they are more time-consuming.

Wordwrap
When keying in your document DO NOT press **ENTER** or **RETURN** at the end of a line as the text will automatically wrap to the next line. Only press **ENTER** at the end of a paragraph or after a heading (or other short line).

Activity
1

Keying in paragraphs

Key in the following Activity, beginning each line at the left margin. This is known as 'blocked paragraphs'. Don't worry about any errors — you can correct them later. Keep the document on screen as you will be using it again for Activity 2.

PROOF-READING   ← press ENTER/RETURN twice

As you complete each task in this new package you must check and edit your work before you print out. Initially, you will find that it is harder to check your work on the screens than it is to check a printed copy but, don't worry; with practice your accuracy and proof-reading skills will soon improve. At the beginning of your word processing course you may find it difficult to remember the commands to edit your documents but within a few weeks you will find that it begins to feel easier and then you will enjoy the learning process! ← press ENTER twice

It may help you to know that when you have completed your course and sit the exam, you can have a copy of the manual by your side as you work. ← press ENTER twice

This means that if you need to look something up you can, but you will probably find that it is not necessary. ← press ENTER twice

REMEMBER though, no matter how good you are at editing your documents, you must still develop good proof-reading skills if you hope to achieve a keyboarding qualification. If you fail to spot your errors you will not correct them and your printed copies will be inaccurate. ← press ENTER twice

Notice how your cursor moves as you key in.

Keyboard technique:

1 Press the keys gently
2 Some keys are repeater keys!
3 Eyes on source copy as you work

RSA Stage I Abbreviations

The following abbreviations should always be expanded — make sure you can spell the words correctly for your exam.

accom. *	accommodation	*opp(s).* *	opportunity/ies
a/c(s).	account(s)	*rec(s).*	receipt(s)
ack.	acknowledge	*rec.* *	receive
advert(s). *	advertisement(s)	*recd.* *	received
appt(s).	appointment(s)	*recom.*	recommend
approx.	approximately	*ref(s).* *	reference(s)
bel. *	believe	*refd.*	referred
bus. *	business	*resp.* *	responsible
cat(s).	catalogue(s)	*sec(s).* *	secretary/ies
cttee(s).	committee(s)	*sep.* *	separate
co(s). *	company/ies	*sig(s).*	signature(s)
def. *	definite(ly)	*suff.*	sufficient
dev.	develop	*temp.*	temporary
ex.	exercise	*thro'.* *	through
exp(s).	expense(s)	*sh.* *	shall
exp.	experience	*shd.*	should
gov(s).	government(s)	*wh.* *	which
gntee(s).	guarantee(s)	*wd.*	would
immed.	immediate(ly)	*w.* *	with
incon.	inconvenient/ience	*wl.*	will
mfr(s).	manufacturer(s)	*yr(s).*	year(s)
misc.	miscellaneous	*yr(s).*	your(s)
necy. *	necessary	*dr.*	dear

* days of the week (eg *Thurs., Fri.*)	Thursday, Friday
* months of the year (eg *Jan., Feb.*)	January, February
* words in address (eg *Cres., Dr.*)	Crescent, Drive
* complimentary closes (eg *-ffly., scly.*)	faithfully, sincerely

NB Retain other commonly used abbreviations such as *NB*, *etc*, *eg*. Only use the & (ampersand) in company names, not in ordinary text.

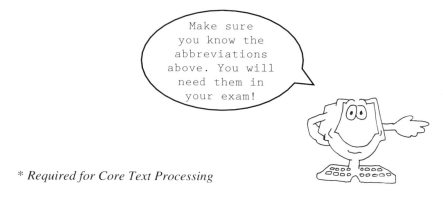

Make sure you know the abbreviations above. You will need them in your exam!

* Required for Core Text Processing

Corrections signs

In addition to expanding abbreviations and correcting words you may have to make other amendments. Study the correction signs below before correcting Activity 2.

New paragraph	⌐ or //
Run on	
Insertion*	∧ with word(s) above or balloon with arrow
Transpose horizontally	∽ or balloon
Transpose vertically	⟂ or balloon
Stet (literally, 'let it stand')	.... with ✓ in margin

* Required for Core Text Processing

Examples

They are going home. ⌐We hope
they have a safe journey.

OR

They are going home. //We hope
they have a safe journey.

They are going home.

We hope they have a
safe journey.

Your records will be returned
as soon as possible.

This should be within the
next fortnight.

Your records will be
returned as soon as
possible. This should
be within the next
fortnight.

this is a new from

this is a new form

her address and name

her name and address

6 7 1

671

16	44
32	50
72	10

44	16
50	32
10	72

Purple   A9
Pink   A3
Black   A8

Black   A9
Pink   A8
Purple   A3

~~closest~~
Go to the ~~nearest~~ shop.

Go to the nearest shop.

7

REMEMBER to read the instructions below first and then follow them to complete Activity 2.

Moving your cursor

$$\uparrow$$
$$\leftarrow \quad \rightarrow \qquad \text{main cursor keys}$$
$$\downarrow$$

CTRL ← (hold down **CTRL** and press ←) one word left
CTRL → (hold down **CTRL** and press →) one word right
HOME ← (press **HOME** then ←) beginning of line
HOME → (press **HOME** then →) end of line
END end of line
HOME HOME ↑ (press **HOME** twice then ↑) beginning of document
HOME HOME ↓ (press **HOME** twice then ↓) end of document

NB You can also use your **PAGE UP** and **PAGE DOWN** keys.

Editing text

Deleting

DEL deletes at cursor position
BACKSPACE (←) deletes text to left of cursor
CTRL BACKSPACE deletes word at cursor position
CTRL END deletes from cursor to end of line

Inserting and overtyping

You are usually in insert mode. Position cursor where you want to insert text and key in. To change to typeover mode, press **INS** key; text keyed in will overtype (and delete) existing text. Press **INS** key to return to insert mode.

Reforming text

Edited text will automatically re-format when you move cursor.

Joining paragraphs

Position cursor immediately after full stop at end of preceding paragraph, press **DEL** twice (to delete two hard returns) and press space bar twice to leave two spaces after the full stop.

Dividing paragraphs

Position cursor on first character of new paragraph, press **ENTER** twice.

Printing

1   Make sure printer is set up correctly
2   Press **SHIFT + F7** (print)
3   Select **1** (full document) or **2** (page)

Saving a document

1   Press **F7** (save document?); type **Y** for Yes (document name?); key in name of
    document, eg **A:docname**
2   Press **ENTER** (exit WordPerfect?), type **N** for No to clear screen or **Y** to leave
    WordPerfect.

Editing text, proof-reading, printing and saving

Now use the commands opposite to correct any errors you have made and also
amend as indicated below. You may need to refer to page 7 to complete the
amendments. Name your document **Act 2.**

```
PROOF-READING
                        activity
             carefully
As you complete/each  task /in this  new package  you must check and
edit your work before you print out.  Initially, you will find
that it is harder to check your work on the screen than it is
                                          not
to check a printed copy but, don't worry, with practice your
accuracy and proof-reading skills will soon improve. [At the
beginning of your  word processing  course you may find it
difficult to remember the commands to edit your documents but
within a few weeks you will find that it begins to feel easier
and then you will enjoy the learning process!

It may help you to know that when you have completed your course
and sit the exam, you can have a copy of the manual by your side
as you work.                              instructor

This means that if you need to look something up you can, but you
will probably find that it is not necessary.

REMEMBER though, no matter how good you are at editing your
documents, you must still develop good proof-reading skills if
you hope to achieve a keyboarding qualification.  If you fail to
spot your errors you will not correct them and your printed
copies will be inaccurate.
```

Begin
each para-
graph at the
left margin.
This is called
'blocked para-
graphs'.

```
Follow this routine:

Proof-read screen copy and edit
Print document
Proof-read print-out
Edit/reprint if necessary
Check with answer
Save document
In class, hand in for marking
```

Function keys

Keys **F1-F12** are function keys which may be used on their own or with three other keys: **CTRL**, **ALT** and **SHIFT**. When using **CTRL**, **ALT** or **SHIFT** you must hold these keys down and then press the appropriate function key. This will be indicated with a plus sign, eg **SHIFT + F8**.

Justification on/off

WordPerfect automatically *justifies* text. This means having an even right-hand margin.

To switch off justification, ie to give a ragged or uneven right margin, position cursor at top of document, press **SHIFT + F8** (format), **1** (line), **3** (justification), **1** (left justify only). Press **F7** to return to your document.

Switching off/exiting WordPerfect

1   Press **F7** (exit)
2   Save your work (if necessary)
3   Press **Y** to exit WordPerfect
4   At **C:/** or opening screen remove disk from drive
5   Carefully place disk in disk case
6   Select **PARK HARD DISK** from menu or if at **C:/**, type **PARK** and press **ENTER**
7   Switch off machine

Depending on how your computer is set up, steps 6 and 7 above may vary.

Keying in, proof-reading, editing text and saving

Key in the following Activity with all the deliberate errors and abbreviations, using a ragged right margin. Name your document **Act 3**.

TYPING FROM MANUSCRIPT

Some of the exam tasks will be in the form of manuscript - that is handwritten copy. this is not as easy to follow as typescript so you must always read it thro' carefully 1st.

REMEMBER to include all normmal grammatical punctuation as shown in the copy. As you already know, you shd. leave one space after all punctuation marks except at the end of a sentence when you should leave too.

If quotation marks is used they may be in the 'single' or "double" form as shown here. Fllow the copy but REMEMBER to type the marks close up to the word. The apostrophe may be used in different ways - it may denote possession, eg the student's work, the boys' lessons or it may represent time, eg 5 o'clock, 3 weeks' holiday, one week's pay. Sometimes the apostrophe is used to show omission, eg don't, can't, won't. When it is used in this way type the words out in full unless they are quoted as direct speech.

Confusion sometimes arises over the use of the hyphen & the dash. Leave no space when you type the hyphen, eg part-time but REMEMBER to leave a clear space - like this - for the dashes.

If you come across a foreign or unfamiliar word you must type it carefully. To help you in yr. exam such words wl. be clearly legible or written at the side in the box.

Some word may be abbreviated, eg shd. for should and wl. for will and these will be followed by a full stop.

You must always type these words out in full and omit the full stops.

Other words may contain deliberate keying in errors for you to corect. There may be obvious errors of agreemen and punctuation, including apostrophes. To make it easier for you these words will be indicated for you in the draft by a circle around the incorrect word.

REMEMBER Still press ENTER/RETURN twice after the heading and between paragraphs.

Operator - please save this document but do not print it yet.

REMEMBER to read the instructions below first and then follow them to complete Activity 4.

Retrieving a document

1   With a blank screen press **SHIFT + F10** (retrieve)
2   Key in **a:(docname)** and press **ENTER**

Codes

If you change the layout of your document, eg switching off justification, WordPerfect inserts codes to determine how your text looks both on the screen and at the printer. However, these codes are not shown in the normal editing screen. Sometimes unwanted or misplaced codes can cause problems so it is useful to be able to see these codes when necessary.

Revealing codes

To reveal codes, press **F11** or **ALT + F3** (repeat to return to normal editing screen). This divides the screen into two parts. The top part is the normal editing screen while the lower part displays the same text, accompanied by the codes it contains.

Justifying text

To switch on justification, position cursor at top of document and press **SHIFT + F8**, **1**, **3**, **4** (full justification). Press **F7** to return to document.

OR

Reveal codes (**F11** or **ALT + F3**) and delete **JUST LEFT** code.

```
Computer technique:

As you know, when you key in you
must keep your eyes on the source
copy, BUT always watch the screen
as you use the computer commands.
```

Retrieving, justifying, proof-reading and editing

Retrieve Activity 3, correct the errors, expand all abbreviations, amend as shown below and justify the right margin. Print and save. Name your document **Act 4**.

```
TYPING FROM MANUSCRIPT

Some of the exam tasks will be in the form of manuscript -
that is handwritten copy. (this) is not as easy to follow as
typescript so you must always read it thro' carefully 1st.
                                                        first

REMEMBER to include all normal grammatical punctuation as
shown in the copy.  As you already know, you shd. leave one
space after all punctuation marks except at the end of a
sentence when you should leave too. (2 spaces)
                                  two

If quotation marks (is) used they may be in the 'single' or
"double" form as shown here. (Fllow) the copy but REMEMBER to
type the marks close up to the word. //The apostrophe may be
used in different ways - it may denote possession, eg the
student's work, the boys' lessons or it may represent time, eg
5 o'clock, 3 weeks' holiday, one week's pay.  Sometimes the
apostrophe is used to show omission, eg don't, can't, won't.
When it is used in this way type the words out in full unless
they are quoted as direct speech.

Confusion sometimes arises over the use of the hyphen & the
dash.  Leave no space when you type the hyphen, eg part-time
but REMEMBER to leave a clear space - like this - for the
dashes.
                                            always
If you come across a foreign or unfamiliar word you must/type
it carefully.  To help you in yr. exam such words wl. be
clearly legible or written at the side in the box. (a)
                                              S
Some word may be abbreviated, eg shd. for should and wl. for
will and these will be followed by a full stop.
You must always type these words out in full and omit the full
stops.

Other words may contain deliberate keying in errors for you to
(corect).  There may be obvious errors of agreemen and    lt
punctuation, including apostrophes.  To make it easier for you
these words will be indicated for you in the draft by a circle
around the incorrect word.
```

```
Follow this routine:

Proof-read screen copy and edit
Print document
Proof-read print-out
Edit/reprint if necessary
Check with answer
Save document
In class. hand in for marking
```

2 Displaying Text

REMEMBER to read the instructions below first and then follow them to complete Activity 5.

Changing line spacing
1 Press **SHIFT + F8** (format)
2 Select **1** (line) and **6** (line spacing)
3 Type **2** for double line spacing and press **ENTER**
4 Press **F7** to return to document

Spellcheck
1 Position cursor on word or page to be checked or anywhere for full document
2 Press **CTRL + F2** (spell) and select either **1** (word), **2** (page) or **3** (document)
3 Cursor moves to any word mis-spelt and gives alternatives
4 Correct by typing letter next to suggested word. If correct word is not given, select **4** (edit) and make correction yourself, then press **F7** to continue
5 If cursor stops at a proper noun (ie a person's name or a place) or a correct word, which WordPerfect does not recognise, select **2** (skip)
6 To stop spellcheck part way through, press **F1**
7 When spellcheck is complete, the number of words in document is given and a message tells you to press any key to continue

REMEMBER: the spellcheck can only check the spelling of words. You must still proof-read your work carefully for words missed out, extra words inserted and alternative spellings — *there/their, male/mail,* etc.

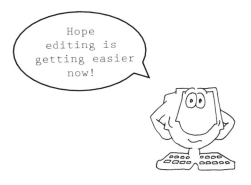

Double line spacing and spellcheck

Key in and amend the Activity below in double line spacing with a ragged right margin. Use the spellcheck before you print and save your work. Name your document **Act 5.**

WORD PROCESSING — spaced caps

Word Processing is very popular in offices today because it means that documents can be produced easily & quickly.

A computer keyboard is used to key in information (data) & this can be stored on a disk for future use — there is no longer any need for boring repetition of work. Once a document has been saved on disk it can be amended & recalled as necy. prior to printing. // There is obvious advantages to the employee & employer. The keyboard operator is able to produce work to a very high standard, use a range of functions to enhance the display, amend documents quickly & easily so the work becomes more interesting & less stressful.

From the employers point of view, more work can be produced to a higher standard in a shorter period of time & staff morale is always higher as they have more job satisfaction.

```
Remember the routine:

Use spellcheck
Proof-read screen copy and edit
Print document
Proof-read print-out
Edit/reprint if necessary
Check with answer
Save document
In class, hand in for marking
```

15

Remember to read the instructions below first and then follow them to complete Activity 6.

Emphasising text (before keying in)

bold	**F6** (before and after text)
underline	**F8** (before and after text)
italics	**CONTROL + F8, 2, 4** (before and after text)
large print	**CONTROL + F8, 1, 5** (before and after text)
very large print	**CONTROL + F8, 1, 6** (before and after text)
extra large print	**CONTROL + F8, 1, 7** (before and after text)
centre	**SHIFT + F6**
right align	**ALT + F6**
different fonts (pitch)	**CONTROL + F8, 4**, select fonts required (then return to original font)

CLOSED CAPITALS
S P A C E D   C A P I T A L S
Initial Capitals

If you can use the commands below, tick the OKAY column. If not, revise them, then tick the RECAP column.

QWERTY CHECKLIST				
You should now be able to:		OKAY	RECAP	DATE
	page			
Switch on/load WordPerfect	4			
Create a new document	4			
Edit text	8			
Print a document	8			
Save a document	9			
Switch justification off	10			
Switch off/exit WordPerfect	10			
Retrieve a document	12			
Switch codes on/off	12			
Switch justification on	12			
Change line spacing	14			
Use spellcheck	14			

Emphasising text/headings
Key in the following Activity and then print and save your work. Name your
document **Act 6**.

TYPES OF HEADINGS — *bold & very large*

DISPLAY STYLES — *bold, underline or large*

*The MAIN HEADING is usually displayed at the top of a document
and is given more emphasis than any other headings - CLOSED
CAPITALS or S P A C E D   C A P I T A L S (one space between
letters and 3 between words) may be used. If the main heading
is followed by a sub-heading, as shown above, it is separated
from the sub-heading by a ~~clear~~ line space.* — *italics*

SHOULDER HEADINGS WITHOUT UNDERLINE — *bold*

These headings may be typed in capitals (upper case) without the
underline or as shown (below)

Shoulder Headings with Underline — *bold + underline*

In this case the shoulder heading has initial capitals &
therefore needs the underline to give emphasis to the text.

LINE SPACING FOR SHOULDER HEADINGS — *bold*

If single line spacing is used you shd. press RETURN/ENTER twice
after each heading and at the end of each paragraph. // If double
line spacing is used you shd. press RETURN/ENTER twice after the
heading\main and at the end of each paragraph but only once after
each shoulder heading.

Paragraph Headings.   These are part of the paragraph. If the
paragraph ends with a full stop, REMEMBER to leave 2 spaces
before the new sentence begins.

Paragraph Headings   Sometimes the paragraph heading isn't
followed by a full stop even when it is followed by a new
sentence.
You must still leave 2 spaces before the sentence as the full
stop is 'implied'.

Yet another style of paragraph heading has the first few words
of the sentence underlined, as here. It is, therefore, not necy.
to leave 2 spaces. *Shown*

Don't
underline final
punctuation!

17

Personal letter (Core Text Processing Students only)
Key in the sample personal letter below with a ragged right margin and then print and save your work. Name your document **Act 7**. Finally, study the notes on the next page and then type an envelope to go with your letter.

Chapston House
500 Beverley Rd.
KINGSTON
KA1 7QK

(date for today)

Core Text Processing Students
Ace Training Academy
3 Westlands Rd.
NORWICH
NR10 3LL

Dear Students

CORE TEXT PROCESSING

Thank you for the interest you (has) shown in my ~word~ processing book and the effort you have made to complete the activities. (so far)

The Core Text Processing exam consists of three tasks to be completed in one hour - a personal ~~business~~ letter (to be dated), an envelope to go w. the letter (wh. may be produced on a computer or typewriter keyboard) and a bus. document in continuous text (in single or (doubel) line spacing).

To be successful ~in the exam~ you must complete all the ~~exam~~ tasks in one hour, proof-read carefully, ~~and~~ edit your work if necy. and be consistent in your style of presentation. (it) is much quicker and easier to use the fully blocked layout as shown in this activity.

You ~~wl~~ *will* find it useful to look at the activities in this book on courtesy titles ~(and open punctuation)~ before you begin your first exam paper.

Keyboarding (are) a very useful skill to develop and I hope you *will* ~~wl~~ continue with the remainder of the activities and wish you good (good) luck in your exam.

Yours s_____

Qwerty Keys

Once you have completed Activities 7 and 8, you will be ready to begin working on Core Text Processing exam papers.

18

Envelopes (Core Text Processing students only)

In the exam you will have to produce an envelope (typewriter keyboard) or an address label (computer keyboard) which should be adhered to the envelope.

If you are unable to type an envelope or produce a label on your equipment, you can key in and print the envelope details on a sheet of A4 paper and then cut to label size and stick on your envelope. If you are short of time in the exam, submit your address details on the A4 sheet as this will only incur one penalty for incorrect use of stationery.

Read (but do not type) the notes below as they will help you to produce your envelope/label.

1 Start the name and address approximately halfway down the envelope.
2 Leave a good left margin so that the details are more or less in the middle of the envelope.
3 Each line of the address should be on a separate line.
4 Use blocked display, open punctuation and single line spacing for the details.
5 Follow the copy regarding the use of capital letters and spelling.
6 The post town is usually typed in CLOSED CAPITALS.
7 The postcode is also typed in CLOSED CAPITALS with one space between the two parts of the code.

Activity 8

Envelope (Core Text Processing Students only)

Follow the instructions to produce an envelope/label, using the details below.

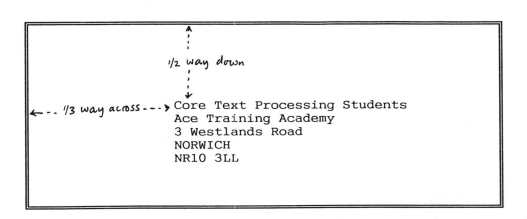

½ way down

←-- ⅓ way across ---→ Core Text Processing Students
Ace Training Academy
3 Westlands Road
NORWICH
NR10 3LL

REMEMBER to read the instructions below first and then follow them to complete Activity 9.

Emphasising text (before keying in)

bold	**F6** (before and after text)
underline	**F8** (before and after text)
italics	**CONTROL + F8, 2, 4** (before and after text)
large print	**CONTROL + F8, 1, 5** (before and after text)
very large print	**CONTROL + F8, 1, 6** (before and after text)
extra large print	**CONTROL + F8, 1, 7**
centre	**SHIFT + F6**
right align	**ALT + F6**
different fonts (pitch)	**CONTROL + F8, 4**, select fonts required (then return to original font)

CLOSED CAPITALS

S P A C E D   C A P I T A L S

Initial Capitals

Emphasising text (after keying in)

If you forget to emphasise your text, you can amend your work afterwards.

To use bold, underline, italics and large print, you will have to 'block' or 'highlight' your text first:

1 Position cursor on first character of text to be emphasised
2 Press **F12** or **ALT + F4** to switch block on
3 Move cursor to end of text to be emphasised
4 Press emphasis command required

To use centre, right align and different fonts, position cursor at beginning of text and press emphasis code required. (With fonts, you must change back to original font size.)

Cancelling a command

If you press any command key(s) by mistake, press **F1** to cancel the command.

Undeleting text

If you delete any text by mistake press **F1** to 'undelete'. WordPerfect stores your last three deletions which you can display on screen and restore if necessary:

1 Press **F1**, last deletion will appear
2 Press **1** (restore) or **2** (previous deletion)
3 If you select **2** (previous deletion), you can scroll back through the deletions by pressing ↑ cursor key
4 When deletion required is 'highlighted', press **1** (restore) or **F1** to cancel

Production: emphasising text/headings

Key in the Activity below within the time allocated, and embolden all shoulder headings. Print and save your work. Name your document **Act 9.**

Please try
and complete
this Activity
within:

15 minutes

Spaced caps, bold, 10 pitch double wide/high

C O M P U T E R   T E R M S

KEYBOARD *(keyboard)*

If you look at your computer you will see that it is similar to a typewriter and uses the standard 'QWERTY' keyboard. The main difference is ~~is~~ the additional keys - special function keys & number pad. You shd. use a gentle keystroking action as you key in as most of the keys are repeater keys.

MONITOR

Display

This is also known as a Visual Unit (VDU). As you input ~~text~~ it appears on your monitor but not necessarily in the format it wl. appear on yr. printout.

INPUT Keying in text is known as inputting. Even though yr. text appears on yr. monitor, as a good keyboard operator, you shd. still keep yr. eyes on yr. source material and not on the screen copy. Proof-read yr. screen copy on completion.

DISKS

There are 2 types of computer disks - floppy & hard disks.

The type you use depends upon yr. computer ~~system~~. Care must be taken when handling & storing disks or they may be corrupted & yr. data lost.

HOUSEKEEPING

This is the term used to describe such activities as deleting unwanted documents, making duplicate copies & renaming documents. It is important to delete unwanted documents on a regular basis because if you do not yr. disk wl. become full & you wl. not be able to save any ~~new~~ work.

PRINTER

This is used to produce a paper copy (hard copy) of the data you have input.

This time read and follow the instructions below for erasing files before you begin Activity 10.

Housekeeping

When you have had a document marked if you are in a class situation, or when you have finished with a document if you are working at home, you must remember to erase that document from your disk. Unless you do this on a regular basis, your disk will become full and you will not be able to save any new work.

Deleting a document/file

1 Press **F5**, type **a:** and press **ENTER** to list files on disk
2 Move cursor to document you wish to delete
3 Select **2** (delete)
4 Type **Y** and document will be deleted
5 To delete other documents, repeat steps 2-4
6 Press **F7** to return to screen

Emphasising text (before keying in)

bold	**F6** (before and after text)
underline	**F8** (before and after text)
italics	**CONTROL + F8, 2, 4** (before and after text)
large print	**CONTROL + F8, 1, 5** (before and after text)
very large print	**CONTROL + F8, 1, 6** (before and after text)
extra large print	**CONTROL + F8, 1, 7**
centre	**SHIFT + F6**
right align	**ALT + F6**
different fonts (pitch)	**CONTROL + F8, 4**, select fonts required (then return to original font)

CLOSED CAPITALS
S P A C E D   C A P I T A L S
Initial Capitals

To come out of Large/Italic Text Press [→] button once twice or however many times you have used an instruction.

Do your
housekeeping
before
Activity 10.

Activity
10

Production: emphasising headings

Key in the Activity below with a ragged right margin and amend as necessary.
Print and save your work. Name your document **Act 10.**

MEASUREMENTS ← (Spaced capitals and large pitch)

Measurements are displayed usually as abbreviations
but you may sometimes find them typed in full. Always
use the same style within each piece of work. ⊘

Useful abbreviations:- (measurement)

ft = foot|feet   in = inch|inches
lb = pound|pounds   oz = ounce|ounces
m = metre|metres   cm = centimetre|centimetres
g = gramme|grammes

Operator - please
embolden; display
in one column
and align
all = signs.

Points to note:-

Never add an 's' for any plural measurement abbreviations, for
example 3 lb, 6 oz, 20 cm ø don't use full stops
after the abbreviations when use open punctuation
(except at the end of a sentence) - 7 ft, 18 in, 1 g.

Always leave a clear space between the amount figure ø the ⊘
abbreviation, for example 7 ft 6 in (except when you're
using the ' for feet and " for inches - 4' 6").

Remember to leave a space either side of the lower case 'x'
when it represents the word 'by' -

20 cm x 30 cm, 6 in x 8 in, 5" x 4". ← Centre and bold.

When typing any measurement abbreviations containing
LITRE, a hand-written looped L (ℓ) shd. be used.
Leave a space after the figure(s) ø then insert the
hand-written L (in matching ink) - 5 ℓ, 16 dℓ. in full
Alternatively, you can type litre but remember to
expand any other measurement abbreviations in the ø
same activity task - 4 litres, 60 decilitres, 25 millilitres. ⊘

Please try
and complete
this Activity
within:

15 minutes

REMEMBER to read the instructions below first and then follow them to complete Activities 11, 12 and 13.

Centring text

Horizontally
Press **SHIFT + F6** and then enter text.

To centre more than one line of text, eg a menu:

1   Press **SHIFT + F8** (format)
2   Select **1** (line), **3** (justification)
3   Select **2** (centre), press **F7** to return to document
4   Key in text to be centred
5   Repeat steps 1 and 2
6   Select **1** (left justify) or **4** (full) as required
7   Press **F7** to return to document

Vertically
1   Position cursor at top of page
2   Press **SHIFT + F8** (format)
3   Select **2** (page), **1** (centre page top to bottom)
4   Press **Y** (yes), then **F7** to return to document

Viewing before printing
Press **SHIFT + F7** (print), **6** (view document) to see what your document will look like when it is printed. This will enable you to check the layout of your work and amend if necessary before you print. Press **F7** to return to normal screen.

Centring text

Key in the Activity below, centring it vertically and horizontally. View your work and amend if necessary before you print and save. Name your document **Act 11.**

Operator - please leave 2 clear line spaces (RETURN 3 times) at points marked ✳

CHAPSTON COLLEGE — *spaced caps. and bold*

Word Processing - September 19--

There are still a few places left
on the following courses:-

Beginners - 5 Week Introductory Course

Monday 7.00 pm - 9.00 pm

Improvers - 5 Week Course

Tuesday 7.00 pm - 9.00 pm

RSA Exam Workshop - 30 Week Course

Wednesday 7.00 pm - 9.30 pm

Enrol early to avoid disappointment

Contact Jan on 0991 86754

or

Call in to Chapston College
Weekdays between 9.00 am - 5.00 pm

Remember the routine:

Use spellcheck
Proof-read screen copy and edit
Print document
Proof-read print-out
Edit/re-print if necessary
Check with answer
Save document
In class, hand in for marking

Production: centring/emphasising text

Key in the following Activity, centring it vertically and horizontally. View your work and amend if necessary before you print and save. Name your document **Act 12.**

Please try and complete this Activity within:

7½ minutes

Production: centring/emphasising text

Key in the following Activity, centring it vertically and horizontally. View your work and amend if necessary before you print and save. Name your document **Act 13.**

Please try and complete this Activity within:

7½ minutes

26

3 Enumeration

Sometimes paragraphs are numbered in order to make them easier to understand. Arabic numbers, letters of the alphabet (with or without brackets) and Roman numerals (upper or lower case) may be used for this purpose. Whichever method you use, always begin at the left margin and leave two spaces after the longest number.

REMEMBER, as you are using open punctuation you do not need a full stop after numbers. Study the following examples before you begin the next Activity.

Arabic numbers

1 Arabic numbers may be displayed as shown here.

2 Notice that the second line of the paragraph begins under the number.

1 Alternatively, you may display Arabic numbers as they are typed here.

2 In this sample the second line of text starts under the first.

Alphabet letters

a Letters of the alphabet may also be used.

b Always follow the copy unless otherwise instructed.

(a) Sometimes alphabet letters are displayed as shown here.

(b) Full brackets, as shown here, may be used or even half brackets, eg a).

Roman numerals

i   For small Roman numerals use lower case letters.

ii   Don't forget to leave two spaces after the longest number.

iii Set a tab two spaces after the longest number.

I   Sometimes upper case letters are used.

II   Study this example carefully.

III Capital i (NOT the letter L or number 1) must be used.

Always use a tab to inset numbered items.

27

REMEMBER to read the instructions below first and then follow them to complete Activity 14.

Tabs

Tab stops are pre-set every 13 mm (0.5 in). To change them:

1   Press **SHIFT + F8** (format), **1** (line), **8** (tab set)
2   Clear existing tabs — **CTRL END**
3   Tap your space bar or cursor key to position tabs, eg for Activity 14, tap three times to allow for the number and the two spaces after the number
4   Press **L** or your tab key to set a left tab or **D** to set a decimal tab stop
5   Press **F7** twice

Numbering paragraphs (indenting first line only)

1   Set a tab stop at required position (**SHIFT + F8, 1, 8**)
2   Type the number of the paragraph
3   Press **TAB** to indent first line only
4   Type paragraph

Remember to
allow two spaces
after the number and
set a tab when using
numbered paragraphs.
DON'T use your
space bar.

Activity 14

Using tabs/courtesy titles

Set a tab and key in the Activity below in double line spacing. Print and save your work. Name your document **Act 14.**

COURTESY TITLES ← (Spaced capitals)

It is usual to use courtesy titles on envelopes & letters. Although you wl. not be expected to produce an envelope in the exam, the rules below will be of help to you when producing bus. letters.

Try to remember the rules:

1   it's usual to address a single lady as Miss & a married lady as Mrs;

2   if, however, you are not ~~safe~~ if the lady (are) ∅ married or not use Ms;

or Esq
3   Mr / is the correct way to address a man (but not both);

5   Messrs is often (use) before the name of a partnership;

4   Rev or Dr is used when it is appropriate;

courtesy
6   do not use / titles for a limited (Ltd) or public limited co. (PLC or plc), impersonal names (York Printers), those beginning w. 'The' (The Spinning Jenny) or when a title is included in a name (Sir Qwerty Keys).

REMEMBER to read the instructions below first and then follow them to complete Activity 15.

Numbering paragraphs (insetting whole paragraph)

1 Set a tab stop at required position (**SHIFT + F8, 1, 8**)
2 Type the number of the paragraph
3 Press **F4** to inset the whole paragraph
4 Press **ENTER/RETURN** at end of paragraph to return to left margin

```
        Make sure you
      know how to set tabs
     and always use them for
    inset items.  It's acceptable
   to indent the first line only
   as in Activity 14 or to inset
     the whole paragraph as in
     Activity 15. Always follow
      the layout shown on your
       copy unless instructed
            otherwise.
```

Using tabs/open punctuation

Key in the following Activity with a ragged right margin. Set a tab stop and use **F4** to inset lettered items. Print and save. Name your document **Act 15**.

O P E N   P U N C T U A T I O N — bold

This is the quickest and easiest way to display your work.   The rules to follow are:

leave 2 spaces
(a)↓ normal gramatical punctuation must still be used;
   m

(b)   full stops are ~~left out~~ of abbreviations,   ✓
      omitted

      eg 10 am;

(c)   leave one space between groups of abbreviations,

      eg Q Keys Esq MA BSc;

(d)   a punctuated open letter has no punctuation at all inserted in the reference, date, name & address of addressee or salutation, nor following the complimentary close;

(e)   where sep. items appear on the same line, however, two clear spaces should be left between the sep. items,

      eg Q Keys Esq Chapston House 500 Beverley Road KINGSTON;

(f)   full stops are omitted after ~~figures~~ numbers in numbered items. ✓

Follow this routine:

Use spellcheck
Proof-read screen copy and edit
Print document
Proof-read print-out
Edit/re-print if necessary
Check with answer
Save document
In class, hand in for marking

Using tabs
Key in Activity 16. Set a tab stop and use **F4** for the numbered items, print and save.
Name your document **Act 16.**

MISCELLANEOUS THEORY — centre

USE OF WORDS AND FIGURES

~~In the exam you wl. be expected to be consistent in the presentation + content of yr. work~~ . If you read thro' this activity before you type it you wl. see that the following rules have been applied :-

1   Aim to use figures throughout each activity EXCEPT –

2   at the beginning of a sentence – use a word;

3   for number one on its own – use a word.

By applying the rules 1, 2 + 3 above you wl. increase yr. chances of success in the exam and, hopefully, be one of the successful students to achieve a pass.

Twenty of the students who used my package last year have written to confirm their exam success + to express their thanks for my help during their course. I was pleased to learn ~~of~~ that 16 of the 20 passed with distinction.

Most of them also expressed ~~continuing~~ an interest in continuing with word processing but they wl. have to apply quickly as ~~15~~ ~~of the~~ 12 places have already been filled.

You shd. always be consistent in the presentation + content of yr. work within each ~~activity.~~ piece of work

Production: using tabs

Key in Activity 17 with a ragged right margin. Set a tab stop and use **F4** for the numbered items, print and save. Name your document **Act 17**.

```
MISCELLANEOUS THEORY
            ←——— leave 2 clear
FRACTIONS         line spaces

i     If you need to use a fraction and it is not available on
      yr. keyboard then use a sloping fraction as follows -
      7/16; 3 1/8; 5 11/12.

ii    Use the solidus (oblique) between the figures (as shown
      above) & remember to leave a clear space after the whole
      number & before the fraction.

DECIMALS

i     Use the full stop key with no space either side for a
      decimal point - 12.54; 0.20; 13.02.

ii    Be consistent with the number of decimal places by adding
      a '0' if necessary - 6.755; 10.950; 17.200 (NOT 6.755;
      10.95; 17.2).

MONEY IN CONTEXT

i     Pounds may be displayed as £5 or £5.00.

ii    Pence may be shown as 10 pence or 10p (no space).

iii   If you have pounds & pence in the same activity use -
      £3.00 and £0.50 (NOT £3.00 with 50p or £3 with £0.50).

MONEY IN COLUMNS

i     Always align figures (units under units) for money in
      columns -

      1,350.00
        100.00
          5.00
```

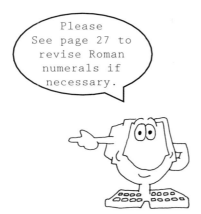

Please
See page 27 to
revise Roman
numerals if
necessary.

4 Re-arranging Text

REMEMBER to read the instructions below first and then follow them to complete Activity 18.

Allocating space

Down the page

Six single lines of typescript measures 25 mm (1 in). To leave 25 mm clear down the page, press **RETURN/ENTER** seven times to leave six clear lines and type on the seventh. To leave clear line spaces, eg nine clear lines, press **RETURN/ENTER** ten times.

QWERTY CHECKLIST			
You should now be able to:	OKAY	RECAP	DATE
page			
Switch on/load WordPerfect 4			
Create a new document 4			
Edit text 8			
Print a document 8			
Save a document 9			
Switch justification off 10			
Switch off/exit WordPerfect 10			
Retrieve a document 12			
Switch codes on/off 12			
Switch justification on 12			
Change line spacing 14			
Use spellcheck 14			
Emphasise text 16			
Block text 20			
Cancel a wrong command 20			
Undelete text 20			
Erase files (housekeep) 22			
Centre horizontally 24			
Centre vertically 24			
View document 24			
Set tabs 28			
Indent paragraphs 28			
Inset paragraphs 30			
Allocate space 34			

Production: allocating space
Key in the following Activity, print and save. Name your document **Act 18.**

Activity
18

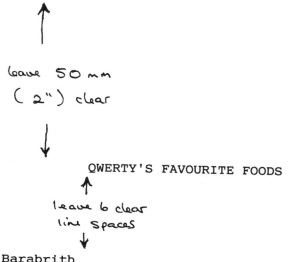

Please try
and complete
this Activity
within:

5 minutes

QWERTY'S FAVOURITE FOODS

Smashing Barabrith

Sticky Toffee Pudding

Death by Chocolate Gateau

Gooseberry Fool Delight

Boozey Fruit Pancake

Lemon Lush Surprise

Spicy Tart

Tipsy Apple Icecream

Operator – please leave 2 clear line spaces between these items

When you
have completed
Activity 18, update
the checklist opposite
and RECAP any commands
necessary.

REMEMBER to read the instructions below first and then follow them to complete Activity 19.

Moving text (cut and paste)

1 Position cursor on first character of text to be moved
2 Press **CTRL + F4**, select text to be moved (**1** = sentence, **2** = paragraph, **3** = page)
3 Select action **1** (**1** = move, **2** = copy, **3** = delete)
4 Position cursor where you want text to be moved to
5 Press **ENTER**

Text to be moved can also be selected by 'highlighting' or 'blocking':

1 Position cursor on first character of text to be moved
2 Press **F12** or **ALT + F4** to switch block on
3 Move cursor to end of text to be moved
4 Press **CTRL + F4** and **1** (**1** = marked block). Continue with steps 3–5 above.

To move a single sentence, paragraph or page, use **CTRL + F4**. To move LESS THAN a sentence, paragraph or page, or MORE THAN a sentence, paragraph or page, use the flexible command **ALT + F4**.

Centring text (after keying in)

Horizontally

To centre text when editing, place cursor at beginning of line to be centred and press **SHIFT + F6** or, for a longer piece of text:

1 Position cursor on first character of text to be centred
2 Press **F12** or **ALT + F4** to switch block on
3 Move cursor to end of text to be centred
4 Press **SHIFT + F6, Y** (yes)

Allocating space/moving text/centring

Retrieve Activity 18 shown below and follow the instructions for moving text to re-arrange the items into numerical order. Finally, centre each line, then print and save. Name your document **Act 19**.

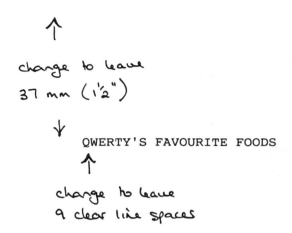

↑

change to leave
37 mm (1½")

↓

QWERTY'S FAVOURITE FOODS

↑

change to leave
9 clear line spaces

↓

4 Smashing Barabrith

5 Sticky Toffee Pudding

8 Death by Chocolate Gateau

1 Gooseberry Fool Delight

7 Boozey Fruit Pancake

3 Lemon Lush Surprise

6 Spicy Tart

2 Tipsy Apple Icecream

To use **CTRL + F4**, select **PARAGRAPH** to include line spaces after the line of text.
To use **ALT + F4**, position cursor at beginning of text and block by moving cursor down to beginning of next line of text to include line spaces.

Allocating space/moving text

Amend Activity 19 by arranging the items into alphabetical order, then print and save. Name your document **Act 20.**

Production: insetting paragraphs

Key in the Activity as shown below, print and save. Name your document **Act 21.**

CARE OF DISKS

Disks shd. be handled carefully or you may find that yr. work has been lost. Although some work may be recovered from a damaged disk it usually means extra work for you & a long wait for an employer!

To save you time & energy follow the guidelines below:-

1   Always hold the disk by the labelled end & insert the disk carefully into the ~~drive.~~ (disk)

2   Do not touch the exposed parts of a disk.

3   Avoid switching yr. equipment on or off while a disk is in the ~~disk~~ drive.

4   Never bend or fold disks.

5   Use a soft tipped pen to write on the label of a disk.

6   Store yr. disks in a ~~suitable~~ suitable dust-proof container when not in use.

7   Keep disks away from magnetic fields such as telephones.

8   You shd. not smoke, eat or drink at yr. workstation.

9   ~~Keep~~ Protect disks ~~away~~ from extremes of temperature.

10   In a work ~~station~~ situation always make a ~~second~~ copy back-up of ~~each~~ disk you use so that if one becomes lost or damaged you wl. still have access to the ~~information~~ ~~data~~ stored on the disk.

Please try and complete this Activity within:

15 minutes

Don't delete this document. You will need it again.

Production: headings

Key in the Activity as shown below with a ragged right margin, print and save.
Name your document **Act 22.**

Activity
22

GLASSARY ← (Centre, underline and large pitch)

Now that you're becoming more proficient w. your word
processing you might be interested in the following
terms :-

Default This is the way yr. w — p — package is
set up, eg your pre-set margins, spacing line etc. You
can ~~change~~ alter the default if necy..   ∅

Copy and Paste This is the method to use when you want
to repeat text within a document.

Cut & Paste   As you'll know this is used to move text
within a document.

Scrolling If yr. ~~document~~ is wider/longer than your ∅
screen you can easily move the text by pressing
the appropriate cursor keys. (or page).

Hard Space By this means you can prevent words from
splitting at the end of a line. A good w — p —
operator always uses the hard space whenever it's
required.
Although it is not essential to use the hard space in your
exam, at this level, your work wd. look much more
professional if you do. Try this for yourself & see.

Please try
and complete
this Activity
within:

10 minutes

Don't
delete this
document. You
will need it
again. REMEMBER
to leave
one clear line
space between
items.

Retrieving/moving text

Retrieve Activity 21, use cut and paste to arrange into the order indicated below and then print and save. Name your document **Act 23**.

CARE OF DISKS

Disks should be handled carefully or you may find that your work has been lost. Although some work may be recovered from a damaged disk it usually means extra work for you and a long wait for an employer!

To save you time and energy follow the guidelines below:-

1   Always hold the disk by the labelled end and insert the disk carefully into the disk drive.

~~1~~ 5 Do not touch the exposed parts of a disk.

~~5~~ 2 Avoid switching your equipment on or off while a disk is in the drive.

4   Never bend or fold disks.

~~6~~ 3 Use a soft tipped pen to write on the label of a disk.

6   Store your disks in a suitable dust-proof container when not in use.

~~7~~ 8 Keep disks away from magnetic fields such as telephones.

~~8~~ 7 You should not smoke, eat or drink at your workstation.

9   Protect disks from extremes of temperature.

10   In a work situation always make a back-up copy of each disk you use so that if one becomes lost or damaged you will still have access to the information stored on the disk.

Always
check your line
spacing after
moving text.

Retrieving/moving text

Retrieve Activity 22, justify the right margin, delete the first paragraph, re-arrange the other paragraphs into alphabetical order and amend as shown below. Print and save. Name your document **Act 24.**

<u>GLOSSARY</u>

~~Now that you are becoming more proficient with your word processing you might be interested in the following terms:-~~

<u>Default</u> This is the way your word processing package is set up, eg your pre-set margins, line spacing etc. You can change the default if necessary.

<u>Copy and Paste</u> This is the method to use when you want to repeat text within a document.

<u>Cut and Paste</u> As you will know this is used to move text within a document.

<u>Scrolling</u> If your document is wider/longer than your screen you can easily move the text by pressing the appropriate cursor or page keys.

<u>Hard Space</u> By this means you can prevent words from splitting at the end of a line. ⌐A good word processing operator always uses the hard space whenever it is required. Although it is not essential to use the hard space in your exam, at this level, your work will look much more professional if you do. ~~Try this for yourself and see.~~

<u>formatting</u> This is the setting up of a document or a disk. New disks must be formatted or else you wl. not be able to save yr. work on them.

Names, dates, money items/measurements etc shd. not be split at line endings.

When moving
these paragraphs, use
CTRL + **F4** and select **PARAGRAPH.**
This will include the underline
code at the beginning. Move cursor
to required position (press **HOME**
3 times then ← to ensure cursor is
before any underline codes on that
line) then press **ENTER** to insert
moved text.

5 Changing Layouts

REMEMBER to read the instructions below first and then follow them to complete Activity 25.

Margins
The default (normal setting) for all margins is 25 mm (1 in). Left and right margins may be shown as 25 mm (1 in) or 10 (10 characters = 1 in). Top and bottom margins are shown as 6 (6 lines = 1 in).

To change left and right margins
1   Press **SHIFT + F8** (format)
2   Select **1** (line) and **7** (margins left and right)
3   Type in new margins and press **ENTER**
4   Press **F7**

To change top and bottom margins
1   Press **SHIFT + F8** (format)
2   Select **2** (page) and **5** (margins top and bottom)
3   Type in new margins and press **ENTER**
4   Press **F7**

Hard space
To prevent dates, figures and names splitting at the end of a line, you can use a hard space. When you are keying in, if you notice that you are near the end of a line:

1   Type first word, eg *Mr*
2   Press **HOME** key then space bar
3   Type next word, eg *Smith*. The words *'Mr Smith'* will be kept together.

When you are proof-reading your document, if you notice that words have been split:

1   Position cursor on space between words
2   Delete space — words will be joined together
3   Press **HOME** key then space bar to insert a hard space between words.

Subscripts/superscripts

1   Press **CTRL + F8** (font) and select **1** (size)
2   Select **2** (subscript) or **1** (superscript) as required
3   Type text
4   Press **CTRL + F8**, **3** (normal) to switch off

Activity 25

Changing margins and using hard space

Key in the Activity below with a ragged right margin. Use your hard space where necessary and left and right margins of 15 (37 mm or 1.5 in). Print and save. Name your document **Act 25.**

Don't delete this document. You will need it again.

MISCELLANEOUS THEORY

PER CENT OR %

I   Use either per cent (2 words) or % ~~symbol~~ - 10 per cent; 15 per cent; 30%. ✓

TIME

I   Use the (12- hour) clock w. a full stop between the hours and minutes and a space before am/pm - 8.30 am, 10.15 pm.

II   Alternatively, use the 24-hour clock with no full stop between the minutes and hours - 0830 hours, 2215 hours.

III Whole hours may ~~also~~ be shown using the abbreviation 'of the clock' - 5 o'clock, 10 (o'clock)

SUBSCRIPTS AND SUPERSCRIPTS

I   (subscripts) are characters wh. (is) typed half a ~~line~~ (character) space below the normal line of text - ✓

     H_2O, H_2SO_4

II   Superscripts are ~~special~~ characters which are (type) half a line space above the normal line of text -

     $60°$, 25 °C, 85 °F.

III Foreign accents are (aslo) included in this section -

     crêpes, garçon.

Use your computer commands for subscripts and superscripts but insert the foreign accents by hand to match your printer ribbon.

CLAIT notes (CLAIT students only)

Key in the notes below in single line spacing with a ragged right margin, print and save. Name your document **Act 26**.

```
                              CLAIT

The latest RSA Computer Literacy and Information Technology
scheme is suitable for anyone who is interested in using
computers and information technology and wishes to gain a
basic qualification.

As information technology is so much a part of our lives
today, it is important to have a basic knowledge of computer
hardware/software.

The RSA CLAIT scheme covers a number of different information
technology applications including word processing.  If you are
interested in the word processing application you should
attempt this activity as it covers all the basic requirements.

To be successful in this element of the scheme you must
complete an assignment of 150-200 words in 2 hours, with no
more than 3 data entry errors and be able to carry out the
whole range of functions shown below:-

Use keyboard/printer/disk storage system
Key in/centre/embolden text/print/save text
Retrieve/insert/delete/replace words
Retrieve/insert/delete paragraphs
Alter format - margins/line spacing/justification on/off
Move text
Switch on/off; load/exit WordPerfect
```

44

Retrieving/editing CLAIT notes (CLAIT students only)

Retrieve Activity 26, carry out the amendments listed below, print and save. Name your document **Act 27**.

1   Embolden the heading.

2   Delete the word latest on the first line of the first paragraph.

3   Insert the bracketed item (at work or at home) after ... computers and information technology ... in the first paragraph.

4   Delete the paragraph which starts As information technology ...

5   Set in the paragraph beginning The RSA CLAIT scheme ... by 5 characters at both the left and right-hand margins and justify.

6   Use double line spacing for the paragraph beginning To be successful ...

7   In the listed items replace the words Alter format ... with Change layout ...

8   Move the last line in the list beginning Switch on/off; ... to become the first line in the list.

9   Add the following as the last paragraph

    If necessary, printing may be carried out after the assignment time.

Once you have completed Activities 26 and 27, you will be ready to begin work on CLAIT assignments.

REMEMBER to read the instructions below first and then follow them to complete Activity 28.

Copying text (copy and paste)

1 Position cursor on first character of text to be copied
2 Press **CTRL + F4**, select text to be copied (**1** = sentence, **2** = paragraph, **3** = page)
3 Select action **2** (**1** = move, **2** = copy, **3** = delete)
4 Position cursor where you want text to be copied to
5 Press **ENTER**

Text to be copied can also be selected by 'highlighting' or 'blocking':

1 Position cursor on first character of text to be copied
2 Press **F12** or **ALT + F4** to switch block on
3 Move cursor to the end of text to be copied
4 Press **CTRL + F4** and **1** (**1** = marked block). Continue with steps 3-5 above.

Well done so far! You've already covered most of the computer commands necessary for your exam and will soon be working from exam papers.

Retrieving, changing margins, inserting and copying text

Retrieve Activity 25, change the left and right margins to 20 (50 mm or 2 in) and check your line endings. Insert the text shown below between the paragraphs headed TIME and SUBSCRIPTS/SUPERSCRIPTS. Copy the main heading to the bottom of your document. Print and save. Name your document **Act 28.**

DITTO MARKS

I   Double quotation marks (is) used for repeating ~~phrases~~ words —

3 blue jackets
2 "   "

II   Never use ditto marks for figures or money items.

LINE ENDINGS

I   Do (not) divide names + names + courtesy titles at the end of a line — Mr Keys.

II   Do not divide words + figures or money together —

$380.50, 36 bottles.

Operator — if this does not fit onto one page change the margins to 15 — 10 — thanks

Remember the routine:

Use spellcheck
Proof-read screen copy and edit
Print document
Proof-read print-out
Edit/re-print if necessary
Check with answer
Save document
In class, hand in for marking

REMEMBER to read the instructions below first and then follow them to complete Activity 29.

Paragraphs

Insetting from left margin
1   Set tab stop at required position (**SHIFT + F8, 1, 8**)
2   Press **F4** to inset whole paragraph
3   Press **ENTER** at end of paragraph to return to original left margin.

   OR

You can change your left margin, but you will have to remember to change it back again at the end of the inset paragraph.

Editing text

Changing capitalisation
Text can be changed from lower case to upper case (and vice versa) after keying in.

1   Block text to be changed (**F12** or **ALT + F4**)
2   Press **SHIFT + F3**
3   Select **1** (upper case) or **2** (lower case) as required.

Read through the next Activity carefully before you key in.

Allocating space

Key in the Activity below and retain initial capitals for shoulder headings. Print and save with a ragged right margin. Name your document **Act 29.**

ALLOCATING SPACE — large

Down the Page

(asked)

Six single lines of text when measured represents ≠1" (25mm) so if you are / to leave, for example, 1" clear down the page you shd. press ENTER/RETURN 6 PLUS ONE MORE so that you leave 6 clear lines + type on the seventh.

↑
leave 1" clear (25mm)
↓

Across the Page

If, however, you are asked to leave a space across the page you must consider the pitch you are using. The most common ones are 10 pitch (10 characters to 1") and 12 pitch (12 characters to 1").

To leave a space of 1" across the page you ~~should~~ ~~must~~ tap ⊘ yr. space bar ~~12~~ 10 times if you are using 10 pitch or 12 times if you are using 12 pitch + then set a tab stop or reset yr. left margin / at that point.

← Inset →
by 1"
(25 mm) Blank spaces are often left in this way for the insertion of logos , photographs etc.

REMEMBER to return to yr. original margin after the inset paragraph as ⊬here. (shown)

Operator — please change shoulder headings to caps.

> Retain words and figures as copy.
> Remember: words at the beginning of a sentence and for number one on its own.

49

REMEMBER to read the instructions below first and then follow them to complete Activity 30.

Paragraphs

Insetting from both margins

1 Set tab stop at required position from left margin (paragraph will be inset from both margins by same amount)
2 Press **SHIFT + F4** to inset whole paragraph
3 Press **ENTER** at end of paragraph to return to original margins

OR

You can change your left and right margins, but you will have to remember to change them back again at the end of the inset paragraph.

Insetting from both margins

Key in the Activity below in double line spacing with a justified right margin. Retain initial capitals for paragraph headings. Print and save. Name your document **Act 30**.

Activity 30

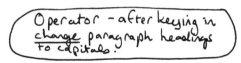

Operator – after keying in change paragraph headings to capitals!

Encouraged by my family & friends I struggled to maintain my life-long diary record and at times nearly gave up. The quality of my entries ~~varied~~ changed over the yrs. as ✓ I moved thro' different phases of my life.

(Inset by 25 mm (1") from both margins)

[Monday Recd. my word/processing exam results today & much to my surprise I have passed w. distinction. I intend to persevere w. this new skill now & aim for Stage II in Sept.. I've noticed in recent job adverts. that secs. w. w—— p—— skills are in demand & can command a high salary. [Tuesday Good news at work. I am to rec. a salary increase next month now that I'm ~~officially~~ a qualified w—— p—— operator. ✓

//It has been an outlet to express my 'literary self' in print over the yrs. & although my entries wl. never shock or ~~even~~ interest the literary world perhaps one day I'll be glad of the records.

Production: allocating space
Key in the Activity below with a justified right margin. Print and save. Name your document **Act 31**.

PAVLOVA ← (Spaced caps.)

This delicious pudding is so ~~easy~~ *quick* to make - why not try it yourself & see! ✓

Operator - please inset last paragraph by 25 mm (1") from each margin - SHIFT F4.

Please try and complete this Activity within:

15 minutes

Leave a space here approx. 50 mm x 50 mm (2" x 2") - change left margin.

Ingredients

3 large fresh egg whites
6 oz caster sugar
1/2 pint whipped cream
12 oz soft fruit
sifted ~~icing~~ sugar ✓

Method

Whisk the whites egg in a large clean bowl until you can turn the bowl upside down without them sliding out (DO NOT OVER-BEAT THE EGGS).
[When the eggs are ready whisk in the caster sugar, approx. 1 oz at a time, & w. a metal tablespoon spoon the mixture onto a non-stick baking sheet forming an 8 inch circle.]

Leave a space here of 63 mm x 25 mm (2½" x 1") - change right margin.

(Use a skewer to decorate the meringue. // Cook the meringue in the oven at 140 °C for one hour & then turn ~~down~~ the oven off. Leave overnight. (in the oven)

To serve Pavlova, remove *from* the baking sheet and top w. cream (whipped) and fruit of yr. choice.

Don't forget to change margins back to original settings after inset paragraphs.

6 Business Letters

Production: business letter notes

Key in the Activity below in double line spacing with a justified right margin. Print and save your work. Name your document **Act 32**.

right align MAIN PARTS OF A BUSINESS LETTER

REFERENCE

This usually consists of the author's initials & the (typists) initials, eg AC/YZ. (Only use a reference if one is quoted.)

DATE

This shd. be typed in the order of the day, month and year, eg 14 May 1991.

SPECIAL INSTRUCTIONS

Any instructions special such as PRIVATE, URGENT, FOR THE ATTENTION OF, are /typed in capitals. /usually

ADDRESSEE

This is the ~~person~~ _individual_ to whom the letter (are) addressed. Apply yr. ✓ courtesy title rules for this item.

SALUTATION/COMPLIMENTARY CLOSE

If a letter begins with Dear Sir(s) it shd. end w. Yours faithfully. If, however, it begins with Dear Mr Smith the letter shd. ~~end~~ _first_ with Yours sincerely. ✓

Operator — please copy main heading to bottom of document.

Remember to **RETURN** twice after main head-ing and at end of each paragraph. Only **RETURN** _once_ after shoulder headings.

52

Business letter/layout
Key in the following Activity with a ragged right margin. Name your document
Act 33.

BUSINESS LETTERS

Business letters are formal letters which are used in most
offices today. All business letters are printed on headed
paper with a copy kept for reference purposes. (The copy may
be a carbon copy, second printout or a photocopy.) In an
office situation it is the usual procedure to type an
appropriately sized envelope/address label.

Reference   ← **press ENTER/RETURN twice**

Today's date   ← **ENTER twice**

Special instructions (eg PRIVATE, URGENT etc)   ← **ENTER twice**

Name of Person
Street
TOWN (in capitals)
County
Postal Code   ← **ENTER twice**

Dear Sir (salutation)   ← **ENTER twice**

LETTER HEADING (in capitals)   ← **ENTER twice**

You should use blocked paragraphs in the fully-blocked letter.
Remember to always leave one clear line space between
paragraphs. ← **ENTER twice**

As every line starts at the left margin in the fully-blocked
letter, it is quicker and easier to type. ← **ENTER twice**

Yours faithfully (complimentary close)
NAME OF FIRM SENDING THE LETTER   ← **ENTER 5 times**

Name of person signing letter
Job of person signing letter   ← **ENTER twice**

Enc or Encs [if enclosure(s) with letter]

You may
handwrite the
instructions
printed in bold
to help with
revision.

Business letter/changing margins/insetting paragraphs

Key in the following Activity with a top margin of 9 (37 mm/1.5 in) and left and right margins of 15 (37 mm/1.5 in). Please justify the right margin. Print and save. Name your document **Act 34.**

Mr M Hussein
10 Hastings Rd.
CAMBRIDGE
CB6 3DQ

Dear Mr H ———

Remember: always date letters and include 'Enc' if necessary.

I was ~~so~~ very pleased to hear from you & to learn about yr. progress w. your studies recent. // I rec. many letters from my students & it always gives me a great deal of pleasure to know how they're enjoying (there) learning w. the help of my books. *or* ~~packages~~

All my current/publications (is) ~~now~~ available from booksellers in your area (list attached) or from my publishers:-

Inset by 1½"
(37 mm)

I hope you will continue with your studies and wish you every success in the future. ~~Please let me know how your progress~~

Yrs. S ———

QWERTY KEYS

Stanley Thornes (Publishers) Ltd
Ellenborough House
Wellington St.
CHELTENHAM
Glos GL50 1YD
(Telephone: 0242 228888)

Business letter/changing margins/insetting
Key in the following Activity with a top margin of 9 (37 mm/1.5 in) and left and
right margins of 15 and 10 (37 mm/1.5 in and 25 mm/1 in). Print and save. Name
your document **Act 35.**

Please send the letter below to T Jackson Esq of
17 Anton Court BEVERLEY East Yorkshire HU17 9AA.
Mark the letter URGENT. You may use a ragged
or a justified right margin.

Dear ———————

EAST Yorkshire Wheelers Christmas Bazaar ← all caps.

As you volunteered at the last cttee. meeting to
organise our Christmas Bazaar I am pleased to
confirm that the following ~~items~~ of memorabilia ✓
are ~~not~~ available for sale:-

Inset by 13 mm (½") please.

1 1923 Rover safety bicycle w. 28"
   wheels.

2 1935 Raleigh Sports lenton ~~cycle~~ bicycle
   w. 21 inch frame & 26" wheels.

3 Sturmey Archer 4-speed hub gear
   built into a dunlop stainless steel
   rim 26" x one inch.

Please find enclosed a copy of the ~~original~~ ~~latest~~ handbook for the ✓
Rover safety bicycle wh. I think you'll find
~~very~~ interesting

Yrs. s———————
~~HUMBERSIDE~~ WHEELERS CYCLE CLUB
EAST YORKSHIRE

R English
Sec.

7 Tabulation

REMEMBER to read the instructions below first and then follow them to complete Activity 36.

Tabulation

If you have to display your work in columns it is normal to leave 3, 5 or 7 spaces consistently between each column. If you set a tab at the start of each column you will find it easier to move across the page from one column to the next.

First of all, clear all previously set tabs. Then look for the longest item in the first column and, starting at your left margin, tap your space bar once for each character and space in that item PLUS 3, 5 or 7 more spaces. Set a tab at this point. Now follow this procedure and set a tab at the beginning of all remaining columns.

Setting tabs

Tab stops are already pre-set every 13 mm/0.5 in (5 spaces). To change them:

1   Press **SHIFT + F8** (format), **1** (line), **8** (tab set)
2   Clear existing tabs — **CTRL END**
3   Tap your space bar or move cursor to position tabs
4   Press **L** for left or **D** for decimal tab
5   Press **F7** twice to return to document

Hope you're enjoying Word Processing. It's a useful skill to develop!

56

Tabulation

Key in the following Activity with a ragged right margin and display the columns as explained on the previous page. Print and save. Name your document **Act 36.**

COMMONLY MIS-SPELT WORDS

<u>Abbreviations</u>

Employers like to ~~shorten~~ ^{abbreviate} words to save them time ✓ when writing out a draft document. When you ~~type~~ the document, you must type the abbreviated words out in full & spell them correctly. Although you ~~may~~ can use a dictionary it is ~~better~~ to make a note of the most commonly used abbreviations & to learn the ✓spelling of ~~them~~ them. (correct)

The following abbreviations are ~~usually~~ ^{often} mis-spelt:—

accomm	accommodation	misc	miscellaneous
advert	advertisement	recom	recommend
bus	business	rec	receive
def	definite	sep	separate
cttee (s)	committee (s)	temp	temporary

(Accommodation) & Sep. are the 2 words most employees cannot spell — make sure you can spell them.

```
Remember the routine:

Use spellcheck
Proof-read screen copy and edit
Print document
Proof-read print-out
Edit/re-print if necessary
Check with answer
Save document
In class, hand in for marking
```

Production: tabulation

Key in the following Activity, *remembering to align decimal points*. Print and save. Name your document **Act 37.**

Please try and complete this Activity within:

15 minutes

STATIONERY

You wl. find that when you decide to buy yr. own/stationery you'll have a stock! // Paper is ~~very~~ expensive to buy so ~~remember~~ to be economical when working either at ① home or at work. [Study the table below & remember to the cost next time you waste a sheet of paper.

SIZE	QUANTITY	QUALITY	PRICE
A4	500 sheets	Bond	£8.70
A5	500 "	"	£5.50
A4 } Continuous	2000 "	"	£12.00

Production: tabulation

Key in the following Activity, print and save. Name your document **Act 34.**

Please try and complete this Activity within:

15 minutes

EXAM SUCCESS ← (Spaced caps)

To pass the Royal Society of Arts Stage I exam, you must fulfil all the criteria listed below.

	PRODUCTION	ACCURACY	PRESENTATION
TARGET	4 tasks	4 tasks	4 tasks
CONSTRAINTS	1½ hours	7 errors	5 errors

If you hope to achieve a distinction in yr. exam you must have no more than **2** accuracy errors and **2** presentation errors.

Operator — please use RSA instead of Royal Society of Arts and use a sloping fraction for 1½.

58

Business letter/ tabulation
Key in the following Activity with a top margin of 6 (25 mm/1 in), bottom margin of 3 (13 mm/0.5 in) and left and right margins 12 (30 mm/1.2 in). Please justify the right margin and mark the letter URGENT. Print and save. Name your document **Act 39.**

Can you spot the missing item?

Our Ref ~~JE~~ ^TL^/WP/aut91

Ms Helen Scott
114 Abbey Road
HULL
HU10 7HH

Dear Ms Scott

Word Processing - September 19-- — *closed caps & underline*

Thank you for yr. enquiry about word processing at the Professional Training Academy.

Inset 25 mm (1") from left margin

RSA STAGE I EXAM CLASS — *underline*

DAY   FROM   TO

Tues   9.30am   11.30 am
Thurs   7.15 pm   9.15 pm

The duration of the course is two hours per week for 15 weeks.

already
As you ~~already~~ have Stage I Typewriting Skills you may join the ~~RSA I exam~~ class. In this class you will learn all the basic word processing functions of WordPerfect 5.1 and cover general display work & bus. documents such as letters and memos. [On yr. course you will work thro' a learning package to help you dev. new skills leading to a ⟨recognised⟩ nationally word processing qualification.

this para. is double line spacing

I look forward to meeting you in September when the new classes ⟨begins⟩.

inset 10 spaces from both margins

Yrs. s _____

Trudi Laubscher
Word Processing Trainer

59

8 Memoranda

Business memo/layout

Key in the following Activity, print and save. Name your document **Act 40.**

Leave two spaces after each heading.

```
MEMORANDUM

                              Set a tab
                              ↓
From   Supervisor             Ref   AC/DI

To   All WP Operators         Date   (today's)


Office Memoranda

Memos  are  messages  from  one  person  to  another  in  the  same
organisation.  They tend to be more informal than letters as they
are not sent out in the post.

The layout of the memo varies according to the 'house rules' of
the organisation.

Points to remember:-

(a)   no salutation or complimentary close;

(b)   Body - usually in single spacing;

(c)   blocked paragraphs must be used consistently;

(d)   Tone  Much more informal than a letter.
```

Business memo/layout

Key in the following Activity, print and save. Name your document **Act 41.**

MEMORANDUM
Set a tab
↓
From   WP Tutor

To   All WP Students

Ref   AN/REG

Date   (today's)

This time leave two spaces after the longest heading and block all the items.

Office Documentation

This is a fully-blocked memo and is the easiest to produce.
However, you must always display your work according to the
stationery you are using and your employer's wishes when you are
at work.

Most firms (has) their own/printed stationery for letters
& memos. If you're using a typewriter you
can easily align yr. typing w. the headings printed.
If, however, you (is) using a word processor
you may prefer to produce yr. own master & store ✓
templates for use with bus. documents.// As printed
stationery is so expensive, producing yr. own templates
to use w. plain paper (usually bulk purchased) is far more
cost-effective. Of course, you shd. always be
economical w. any (stationary) you use, whether
you're at work or training.

On of the main advantages of word processing is that
you can edit (correct) yr. work before printing. Don't fall
into the trap of checking & then printing. A well-trained
word processing operator always proof-reads the work
carefully, edits if necy., & then prints. (Developeing) good
good work habits is important as it helps you to do
the job efficiently & professionally. You may not care
if your waste bin is full of used paper at the end of
the day, but wl. your employer adopt the same attitude!
boss.

on completion

61

Production: business memo/insetting from both margins

Key in the following Activity, print and save. Name your document **Act 42.**

> Operator – date for today + inset numbered items 1" (25 mm) from both margins – thanks

MEMORANDUM

From Course Tutor   Ref WG/JE

To All WP Students   Date (today's)

EXAMINATION HINTS

Now that you're more experienced w. yr. WP skills it's time to think about the exam. the (folowing) notes will be of use to you:-

1   Assemble ~~any~~ all the items you need for yr. exam such as your notes (and a dictionary) in advance. I hope

2   On the day of the exam arrive early.

3   Read carefully through the exam paper for meaning and follow all instructions.

4   Apply the techniques and theory you have (learn) on your course as you (you) work thro' the paper.

5   If in doubt about the layout follow the exam copy

6   Check that you have followed all instructions for each task on the exam paper eg to justify text and change to double spacing.

7   Proof-read all tasks on completion and (cor,rect) errors carefully. You only have a limited amount of paper - not enough to print out each task twice. You will lose marks for presentation if y. print out on the back of a task.

8   Remember yr. timing - you must complete all tasks if you hope to pass.

9   Finally, don't panic - the key to success is to keep calm & think before you type.

9 Adjusting Line Length

REMEMBER to read the instructions below first and then follow them to complete Activity 43.

Pitch

The default (normal) pitch is set at 10 (ie 10 characters per 25 mm/1 in). If you are using A4 size printing paper there are 82 characters across the page from edge to edge.

Line length

As you already know, the left and right default margins are set at 10 and 10, which leaves you with a 62-character line length. An alternative way of asking you to set new margins is to ask you to adjust the line length, for example:

Adjust line length to 50

1   Width of paper (82) minus line length required (50) = 32
2   Divide 32 between left and right margins (32 ÷ 2 = 16)
3   Press **SHIFT + F8** (format)
4   Select **1** (line) and **7** (margins left and right)
5   Type in new margins (16 and 16) and press **ENTER**
6   Press **F7**

**Activity
43**

Adjusting line length/leader dots

Key in the following Activity in double line spacing and inset the numbered items 37 mm (1.5 in) from left margin. Adjust the line length to 50 characters, print and save. Name your document **Act 43**.

LEADER DOTS ——— leave 1" (6 lines) clear after the heading

[Apply the rules following if you have to type leader dots:–]

[You may not come across leader dots in yr. exam but you may have to use them in a work situation. Leader dots are typed as a line of full stops continuous used to help guide yr. eyes from one column to another.]

i) leave a space after the text before typing the leader dots;

ii) if an item extends to more than one line, the leader dots must be typed on the last line.

Production: adjusting line length/footnotes

Key in the following Activity and adjust the line length to 60 characters, print and save. Name your document **Act 44.**

FOOTNOTES ◄ — Spaced caps

3 clear lines

Footnotes are notes generally at the foot of the text & provide additional information about an item in the text. ✓

always
They are typed in single spacing, w. one clear line space between each footnote.

Alphabet letters & Arabic figures are often used for footnote symbols today but the asterisk (*) is the most commonly used letter symbol. // In the text the symbol ✓ shd. be a superscript, except for the asterisk (*), wh. is already a raised character. [You may not come across footnotes in yr. exam but you may have to use them at work so please read thro' these notes so that you know how to use them if necy..

Double line spacing please & justify the right margin.

Please try and complete this Activity within:

10 minutes

The footnotes and leader dots Activities are optional. Only complete them if you have the time.

Leader dots/footnotes

Key in Activities 45 and 46 on one page, print and save as one document.
Name it **Act 45.**

SPARKLERS HEALTH AND BEAUTY CLINIC — large pitch

WE ARE PLEASED TO ANNOUNCE OUR

leave 2
clear line spaces

SPECIAL SUMMER RATES — bold

for all weekends in

JUNE, JULY AND AUGUST — italics

```
Single room ...... £79.50
Double room ...... £119.50
Family room ...... £149.00
```

> Centre each line and remember to leave one clear space before and after the line of leader dots.

I wish/do not wish[1] to attend the Annual Christmas Dinner and
Dance at Chapston House on 20 December.

I enclose my cheque[2] to the value of £   for tickets.

Name ....

Address ....

....

....

[1] Delete as necessary

[2] Please write your name and address on the back

> Follow copy for the footnote symbols and note the spacing used.

Production: business letter/adjusting line length/insetting

Key in the following Activity, print and save. Name your document **Act 47.**

> Please send the letter below to Customised Bus. Equipment – 10 Clarendon Rd. Hull HU7 6RX and mark FOR THE ATTENTION OF MRS N STEPHANOPOULOS. Change the line length to 55 and use a justified right margin.

Please try
and complete
this Activity
within:

25 minutes

Dear Sirs

Specialised Office Equipment - Desks ← (Caps)

We have been advised by Geraldine Maguire to ~~contact~~ ~~telephone~~ you ✓ w. regard to purchasing some new furniture|office. In order to accom. our Special Needs students we wish to purchase some new desks. I Could you confirm|please that the dimensions r prices of the ~~following~~ items are still current. ✓

Inset by 5 spaces

MODEL	SIZE	PRICE
WS Executive	3' x 4' x 24 3/4" high	£56.75
WS Classic	3' x 4' x 22 7/8" high	£45.24
WS Standard	3' x 4' x 27 1/4" high	£39.95

We hope to/place an order w. you for six desks on the basis of yr. standard terms of 12½% discount with 30 days' credit. // We look forward to hearing from you by the end of the month.

Yrs. f ——
WENDOVER TRAINING AGENCY

STEVE GOOD
DIRECTOR

Follow
the layout
of the
copy care-
fully.

Production: business letter

Key in the following Activity, print and save. Name your document **Act 48.**

Activity
48

Please try
and complete
this Activity
within:

15 minutes

Operator — please send this letter to
MS L E O'Brian   'The Willows' Gable End
YORK   YO1 3BL & mark PERSONAL
Adjust line length to 45 — thanks.

Dear ———

STAGE I   WP EXAMINATION

I hope you've enjoyed using my ~~learning package~~ WP book & wd. like to take this opp. to wish you every success in yr. examination. [It takes a great deal of determination & patience to work carefully through a learning package. By completing yr. course of study you've not only improved yr. keyboarding skills but also developed some very good life skills.// I hope when you achieve yr. goal & rec. yr. examination results you wl. decide to return to my "Qwerty" way of learning.

You may be interested to know that the following WP books are currently available at yr. local booksellers:-

WP with Qwerty — Stage II) using WordPerfect
WP with Qwerty — Stage III)

I look forward to working w. you again in due course.

Yrs. s———

Qwerty keys

Production: problem-solving/adjusting line length

Key in the following Activity with a ragged right margin, print and save. Name your document **Act 49**.

Operator - please adjust line length to 55

If you've worked carefully thro' ALL the ~~activities~~ *tasks* in this ☑ book you wl. have had suff. practice to think seriously about the exam. W. all the exp. you have gained on this course you shd. by now be feeling ⌃ with yr. word processing ⟨skills⟩
⟨confident⟩

Don't worry if you have had to repeat any activity, complete some of the supplementary\optional activities or even refer to your machine manual occasionally - this is all part of the natural learning process.
                                    3
       ←——— please leave ⁄ line spaces
PROBLEM SOLVING ⌐ spaced caps

If anything ⟨go⟩ wrong with yr. work - DON'T panic or delete yr. document, there is usually a very simple solution.⌐

⌐Read the notes below as they may help you next time you encounter a problem on your computer.

DISK FAULT If there is a disk fault, an appropriate message will be displayed on yr. screen. ⟨if⟩ you are working on a document save yr. work at this point (to a new disk if necy.). Try to copy *the files* ~~work~~ from yr. faulty disk to a new one & then reformat yr. faulty disk. If the disk wl. not reformat you wl. have to throw it away.

HELP If you exp. any difficulties w. yr. computer commands use the F3 key for help - see HELP in the instruction section *at the back of this book.*

LAYOUT If yr. text looks lined up on the screen but isn't lined up on the printout, reveal yr. codes and check there ⟨is⟩ no unwanted codes and that you've ⟨use⟩ tab/F4/SHIFT F4 correctly (DO NOT use yr. space bar to inset text). Viewing yr. document before printing will show you ⌃ what it wl. look like when printed ~~out~~.   ⟨exactly⟩

PRINTING If yr. printer prints 'garbage ' make sure that the correct printer is selected and, if necy., check yr. printer sharer (if there is more than one computer connected to yr. printer). *If, however, yr. printer does not print at all do not repeat yr. printing commands. Instead, select* ⟨F7 (print),⟩ ⟨SHIFT +⟩ *4 (control printer) + follow the screen prompts.*

Well done! You've worked hard so far and deserve to do well in your exam.

Make sure you know your abbreviations and manuscript signs as you cannot take handouts into the exam with you.

QWERTY CHECKLIST			
	OKAY	RECAP	DATE
You should now be able to:			
page			
Switch on/load WordPerfect 4			
Create a new document 4			
Edit text 8			
Print a document 8			
Save a document 9			
Switch justification off 10			
Switch off/exitWordPerfect 10			
Retrieve a document 12			
Switch codes on/off 12			
Switch justification on 12			
Change line spacing 14			
Use spellcheck 14			
Emphasise text 16			
Block text 20			
Cancel a wrong command 20			
Undelete text 20			
Erase files (housekeep) 22			
Centre horizontally 24			
Centre vertically 24			
View document 24			
Set tabs 28			
Indent paragraphs 28			
Inset paragraphs 30			
Allocate space 34			
Move text 36			
Centre existing text 36			
Change margins 42			
Use hard space 42			
Use sub/superscripts 42			
Copy text 46			
Inset from left margin 48			
Change capitalisation 48			
Inset from both margins 50			
Produce column work 56			
Adjust line length 63			

Please update your checklist next and recap any commands necessary.

If you feel confident with your work, turn to page 93 and begin your exam practice. If not, work through the Supplementary Activities in the next Section.

Section 2:
Supplementary Activities

Have fun
with the following
Activities if you have
the time, as they will
help you revise all the main
computer commands in this book.
Choose your own names for the
Activities as you save them. As
there are no answers for this
Section, take care
to get them
right!

Ragged right margin

Key in the Activity below with a ragged right margin and amend as necessary.

```
A DAY OFF
```

Mark had looked forward to his ~~day~~ off for weeks. He had ✓
worked ~~very~~ hard during the past few months and a day off work
would be bliss!

He wanted to make the most of his free day so he got up early
and dressed in his black leathers. Over a breakfast leisurely
of eggs & bacon he decided that the plan for the day was NO
WORK BUT LOTS OF PLAY! He strolled down the garden path to
the garage and surveyed his pride and joy, his motorbike. He
had been very secretive about his new toy. he knew that his
parents would not approve so he had kept the bike at a friends
house for several weeks before telling them.

They didn't approve, of course, but by then it was to late as
he was the proud owner.

He had not had the opp. to use the bike as much as he would
have liked. As he and his father worked together they usually
travelled in the car family to work and back each day & in the
evenings he was so busy studying for his future accountancy
exams. As he pushed the bike down the driveway to the road he
was excited at the prospect of testing both the bike and his
skill as a rider. He set off on his ~~journey~~ with the wind ✓
blowing in his face and the sweet smell of freedom in his
nostrils. The bike performed well, accelerating to order, & he
was in a world old of his own. // It was not until the police
car stopped him that he realised he had exceeded the speed limit.
The shame of shock was hard to bear but the hardest pill to
swallow was the fact that he wd. probably have to sell
his pride & joy too pay for the speeding fine.

```
Check your print-out for:

Ragged right margin
Manuscript amendments
```

Justification and double line spacing

Key in the Activity below in double line spacing with a justified right margin and amend as necessary.

Janet looked at herself in the mirror and ~~decided~~ *realised* that the diet

was not working. (she) knew she had a problem - she was overweight

& looked unattractive.

None of her clothes (fit) her comfortably and her sloppy sweater

and baggy slacks didn't hide her expanding waistline. Her mirror

image did little for her self -esteem. She couldn't undersand

what she was doing wrong. She had (following) the Slimming (Clubs)

advice of 'more output, less input ' & yet she failed to lose

weight. Every day she exercised by walking to her shops local

and back. In fact, she had become good friends w. the staff in

the local cake shop - she just couldn't understand it!

Check your print-out for:

Justified right margin
Double line spacing
Manuscript amendments

Emphasising and centring text

Key in the Activity below and centre horizontally and vertically.

PUBLIC AUCTION

leave 4 clear line spaces

P E R S I A N   C A R P E T S

Spaced, bold & large pitch

at

THE CLIFFORD ROOMS, COTTINGHAM — *underline*

on

Sat. 8 April at 3.00 pm

Items include: antiques, silks, kellims, nomadic

Rug sizes available: - 3' x 2' 6", 4 ft x 2', 6'x3'.

operator - be consistent with measurements

Terms: Cash, cheque, credit card

4 clear line spaces

Auctioneers: John Weston and Associates
166 Abbey Road
BARTON ON HUMBER

Telephone: 0652 31389

Check your print-out for:

Text emphasised
Text centred
Space allocated
Consistent measurements

Indenting paragraphs

Key in the Activity below and amend as necessary.

PREPARING FOR WORK — *centre, spaced caps & bold*

Whether you are looking for your first job or hoping to find a better one now that you're updating yr. work skills you need to be well prepared for the whole job process application.

1 Think *carefully* about the type of work you are interested in & be realistic about yr. own capabilities and qualifications.

2 Use any expert advice available (careers teachers or Careers Advisory Service) to help you the type of work best suited too you. ~~decided~~ decide

3 Look in the local ~~magazines~~ *newspapers* for jobs currently available and visit job Centres on a regular basis.

4 Prepare a standard letter of application *in advance* and a CV giving all your personal, educational and career details.

5 If you're lucky enough to be invited for an interview *remember to confirm that you wl. be attending.*

6 Do your homework ~~in advance~~ before attending an interview - find out what you can about the firm and prepare a list of questions

7 Don't overdress on the day - work clothes has to be suitable for the job.

8 Finally, BE YOURSELF. *It's no good starting a job if you cannot cope w. it or if you do not like the people you've to work with.*

Check your print-out for:

Text emphasised
Text centred
Tab to indent paragraphs
Manuscript amendments

Insetting whole paragraphs

Key in the Activity below in double line spacing and amend as necessary.

THE DATA PROTECTION ACT — *centre + underline*

The purpose of this /*relatively* new Act is to protect the individual against the use of information (data) stored about them on computers or processors \ *word* and to enforce the rules for the processing of such information. Computer users & computer bureaux must operate within the law and respect the (right's) of the individual. Operators must pay a registration fee and disclose details of personal information they control#.

1 <u>Data Users</u> are the firms holding + processing personal information in <u>Systems</u> \ *computer*, It's possible to be a data user without even owning a computer If, for example, you've personal information processed on yr. behalf.

2 <u>Computer Bureaux</u> are the ~~organisations~~ *companies* who process information on behalf of ^*other* people. They do not own the data but they do own the (Computor) equipment.

3 <u>Data Subject</u> refers to the individual to whom the personal information relate/s As a result of the (act) all individuals (has) the right to access any information stored on computer about them.

```
Check your print-out for:

Double line spacing
Text emphasised
Text centred
Two spaces after numbers
F4 to inset paragraphs
Manuscript amendments
```

Indenting/insetting paragraphs

Key in this Activity and follow the layout indicated below.

CURRICULUM VITAE — *centre, bold & large pitch*

Name — *caps*

                        Jayne
Maria/Woods

ADDRESS

         20 Claremont Ave.
Westongate
GRIMSBY DN34 4TL

TELEPHONE NUMBER

      0724 95880

DATE OF BIRTH

      15 July 1965

GENERAL HEALTH

      Excellent

MARITAL STATUS

      Married — one son aged 5 yrs.

EDUCATION

      1976 – 1983

Sandsford High School
76 Easton Road
BIRMINGHAM B5 6AS

QUALIFICATIONS

      GCSE – English Language
           – Mathematics
RSA – Typewriting Stage I
      – Shorthand Stage I
      – Office Practice Stage I

WORK HISTORY

      July 1983 – September 1985

Clerk/Typist   *Humber Aerials Ltd 13 South St. Hull HU4 7ED*

PERSONAL INTERESTS

      I enjoy all sports especially badminton and swimming. I am a car owner & have a current driving licence.

REFEREES

      Mr L Hope
Humber Aerials Ltd
13 South Street
HULL HU4 7ED

Mrs D Eastwood
143 Tilworth Road
HULL HU13 OND

Check your print-out for:

Text emphasised
Text centred
Tab to indent lines
F4 to inset paragraphs
Manuscript amendments

Moving text

Key in the following Activity and use cut and paste to re-arrange into the order
indicated below.

Why bother to ~~to~~ take a holiday this yr.? All that saving,
planning & preparation is just more trouble than it's worth and
I'm sure you'd rather forget it and stay home. After all the (the)
sun may shine in the ‾garden‾\back and you may be able to ignore
all those jobs ~~around the house.~~ you have to do.)

(You may even ~~enjoy~~ helping in the garden and spring cleaning yr. ✓
bedroom. Of course, you might change yr. mind and w. the help
of the QWERTY HOLIDAY PLANNER below find that your next holiday
is the best one yet!

~~1~~ 4 Book airport parking.

2   Make sure passport is up to date.

~~3~~ 7 Arrange for foreign currency/travellers' cheques.

~~4~~ 1 Check tickets & holiday insurance.

5   Book pets and any relatives (if necessary) into temp. accom..

~~6~~ 10 Notify relatives/neighbours and leave contact details in
     case of an emergency.

~~7~~ 3 Check and arrange for any vaccinations if necessary.

                home
~~8~~ 11 Check/security.

          ~~magazines~~
9   Cancel ~~newspapers~~ & milk.   ✓

~~10~~ 6 Make out packing list and check suitcases.

~~11~~ 8 Arrange personal first(- a)id and medications.

Check your print-out for:

F4 to inset paragraphs
Manuscript amendments
Text re-arranged numerically

Changing margins and copying text

Key in the Activity shown below in double line spacing and change the margins to 15 (37 mm/1.5 in).

If you have ever lost an ~~expensive~~ item you wl. understand the
(the) feelings of frustration and ~~anger~~ at your inability to immed.
find that item when you want it! If you are lucky, sooner or
later (usually much later) it turns up & all is well for the
moment, or so you you bel..

If yr. lost item doesn't turn up you may have to admit defeat and
incur the exp. of (buy) it again or/ even going without.

Every day lots of misc. items are misplaced (inside & outside) the home from false
teeth to bags full of money. Next time you lose something stop
and consider (it's) worth before get upset and if you ~~are lucky~~
actually ~~enough to~~ find ~~that~~ a bag full of money think carefully before you
act - it might be yr. bag next time!

If you find an item that isn't yours, whatever shd. you do with
it? (if) the (owners) name is inside it may be possible to find the
owner (although there is no gntee.) so that the lost property can
be (return). If you don't have the name of the owner you may
decide to place an advert. in the press local in the hope of
making contact or it may be necy. to visit your local Police
Station and go thro' the official procedures to trace the (owner)

LOST & FOUND PROPERTY — copy to top of doc.

Check your print-out for:

Margins changed
Double line spacing
Manuscript amendments
Text moved
Heading copied

Insetting paragraphs from both margins

Key in the personal letter below and note the difference in layout between this type of letter and a business letter.

```
"Wayside"
11 Rosedale Green
SCUNTHORPE
DN16 3QJ

Tel: 0724  333060        ← date for today please

The Personnel Manager
Moods Fashions Ltd
5 Wilson Gardens
SCUNTHORPE
DN10 9ST

Dear Sir  POST SA/689 - A/cs Department Sec.
          ← heading in caps.
```

I wish to apply for the position of Sec. in your Accounts Department wh. I saw advertised in the Scunthorpe Gazette on (date for last Friday). // As you wl. see from my CV enclosed I have good secretarial qualifications and extensive work exp.. I have recently updated my office skills on a 10 week refresher course at the ~~at the~~ Wendover Training Agency (were) I used modern computer equipment to complete word processing, database and spreadsheet assignments. I enjoyed the course and welcomed the opp. to learn about information technology w. a view to returning to work.

> I feel I wd. be suitable for the ~~job~~ position advertised as I am conscientious, hard working & take a pride in my work. I've always wanted to be employed within a large organisation wh. offers many opps.. I enjoy typing and word processing and (has) a good standard of English. I get on well with most people and I wd. like to be a member of a team. (at any time)
>
> *(inset 13 mm (½") from both margins)*

I am ~~currently~~ available for an interview at any time to suit you. I do hope you consider my application favourably. I look forward to hearing from you.

Yours f _____

Sarah Rodgers (Ms)

Enc

```
Check your print-out for:

Sender's address
Letter dated
Receiver's address
Heading inserted
Manuscript amendments
Paragraph inset from both margins
```

Adjusting line length and tabulation

Key in the business letter below and adjust the line length to 50.

on a day to day basis

Please address the letter below to Messrs G Coates & Sons 9 Risby St. MANCHESTER MI8 6DQ and mark for the attention of Ms Joy Lester. Ref: JF/RS212.

Dear Sirs // Thank you for your/recent letter regarding the use of our recording studios for yr. artists. [At the moment we have 2 bands from America using the studios until the end of May.]

We hope to have some slots free after that ~~time~~ date ✓ & wd. suggest that you contact one of our Studio Managers ~~as soon as possible~~. to make a provisional booking

Inset by 25 mm (1")

Contact	Telephone	Availability
Rod Dann	897065	Mon. - Tues.
Suzie Lake	768492	Wed. - Thurs.
Mike Davies	435671	Fri. - Sat.

We have ~~been~~ in the pop bus. for/over twenty-five yrs. & our clients include some of the biggest and the best in the ~~world~~ pop scene. // We hope we wl. be able to be of service to you and look forward to hearing from you.

Yrs. f———
SOUNDS STUDIOS

Jilly Freeman
GENERAL MANAGER

Check your print-out for:

Line length adjusted
Letter dated
Ref and ATTENTION LINE
Manuscript amendments
Columns inset
Words and figures consistent

Allocating space and tabulation

Key in the business letter below, adjust the line length to 55 and leave 13 mm (0.5 in) clear above and below the inset columns.

Please address the following letter to Miss Mandy Abba of 33 Canongate Ave. Bury Lancs BL9 2BJ and mark it URGENT. Ref DP/TE.

Dear ————

Thank you for your enquiry about our service. [We are pleased to enclose full details of our menus| birthday and price lists. As you'll see the choice is endless & our most popular menus for 18th and 21st ✓ birthday parties are:-

MENU CODE	NUMBER OF ITEMS	MEAL TYPE
FDM/1A	7 items	buffet
FDM/3A	13 "	"
FDM/2A	12 "	"

We can cater for small or large/groups & distance is no problem. We pride ourselves on quality & quantity! // As yr. birthday is only 2 weeks away, yr. early reply wd. be appreciated together w. a small deposit of £25 if you wish to proceed.

We hope to be of service to you and, in the meantime, good luck w. yr. birthday planning. ✓

Yrs. s————
SWIFT CATERERS

D Purdy   MANAGER

Check your print-out for:

Line length adjusted
Letter dated
Ref and URGENT
Manuscript amendments
Space allocated
Columns inset

Section 3:
The RSA Stage I Word Processing Syllabus

The following notes are reprinted from the current RSA Stage I Word Processing Syllabus. Read them carefully before you go on to the practice exam papers in Section 4.

RSA SYLLABUS
Word Processing Stage I

1 Aims
This scheme defines word processing competence as a totality of speed, accuracy and presentation skills. Candidates will therefore be assessed in each of these 3 elements and for award of a certificate must meet the criteria specified for all 3 of them.

The overall aim of the scheme is to test the candidate's ability to meet the word processing requirements of the discerning employer.

2 Target Population
The beginner word processor operator who has a sound command of English and basic numeracy and some knowledge of business practice.

The Stage I scheme tests knowledge and skill at a level suitable as a basis for further development and training and for employment.

3 Assessment Objectives

SECTION A - RATE OF PRODUCTION
Candidates must use their machines to work at a rate of production* adequate to complete 4 single-page business tasks within 1½ hours. Working from handwritten drafts and recalled documents, within the 4 tasks they must produce:-

A.1   Standard letter
A.2   Notice, advertisement etc
A.3   Article, report etc
A.4   3-column table with single line headings
A.5   Continuous text (article, extract etc)

System manipulation includes:

AA.1   LOG ON/START UP the system
AA.2   RETRIEVE previously stored documents
AA.3   USE the insert facility to insert within existing text -

   (a)   single character
   (b)   character string (words and phrases)
   (c)   sentence
   (d)   line-space
   (e)   paragraph

---

* The production rate at this level takes into account time for: system manipulation, organisation of time and materials, scanning, reading, interpreting (including use of context to identify words as necessary), use of styles and conventions, checking and correcting, for the purpose of processing drafts in any context.

AA.4   USE the delete facility to delete

    (a) single character
    (b) character string (words and phrases)
    (c) sentence
    (d) line-space
    (e) paragraph

AA.5   USE the move facility to move paragraphs
AA.6   USE the underline facility to underline

    (a) headings
    (b) words within text

AA.7   USE the centre facility to centre lines
AA.8   JOIN 2 paragraphs
AA.9   SPLIT a section of text into paragraphs
AA.10   REPLACE text

    (a) single character/word with text of same length
    (b) long string with shorter string
    (c) short string with longer string

AA.11   REFORMAT text

    (a) justification
    (b) line length adjusting both margins
    (c) line-spacing

AA.12   SAVE text in a new file
AA 13   INITIATE printout
AA.14   LOG OFF/CLOSE DOWN the system

SECTION B - ACCURACY OF CONTENT

Candidates must use their machines to produce work which, after application of appropriate correction techniques, is accurate in content, including compliance with explicit and implicit instructions about content.

They must:

B.1   INSERT date on letters and memos as appropriate
B.2   CONFIRM facts, eg names, dates, from overt information, without explicit instruction
B.3   INCORPORATE amendments to text:

In keying in task:

(a) deletions with replacement

(b) deletions without replacement

(c) correction signs:

new paragraph [or //

run on ↶

insertion ⅄ with letter(s) or word(s) above or balloon with arrow

transpose horizontally ↶ or balloon with arrow

transpose vertically ꞔꞩ or balloon with arrow

stet ----- with ⊘ in margin

> no
> marginal
> instructions

In recall tasks:

(a) deletions with replacement

(b) deletions without replacement

(c) correction signs:

new paragraph [or //

run on ↶

insertion ⅄ with letter(s) or word(s) above or balloon with arrow

move block - balloon with arrow

> no
> marginal
> instructions

B.4 SPELL abbreviated words correctly (see page 6)

B.5 INSERT SPECIAL MARKS, eg Confidential, Attention line, as instructed

B.6 INDICATE ENCLOSURES as implied in draft

B.7 COPY unfamiliar and/or foreign words from legible text

B.8 PRESENT IN CORRECTED FORM material containing:

(a) obvious keying-in errors

(b) obvious errors of agreement and punctuation, including apostrophes

These will be indicated in the draft by circling the incorrect word(s) and will be confined to one specified recalled task.

SECTION C - PRESENTATION OF WORK

Candidates must use their machines to produce work which, after application of appropriate correction techniques, is effectively presented and in line with current styles and conventions - including compliance with explicit and implicit instructions about presentation. They must:

C.1 USE limited supplies of stationery economically and effectively

Candidates using machines which will not take the stationery provided may use equal amounts of stationery provided by the centre; **a note by the Invigilator must be returned with the worked scripts - see Marking Scheme C.1**. If continuous stationery is used, the pages should be separated before insertion in the candidate's folder.

C.2 PRESENT work to fit onto an A4 page

C.3 ENSURE CONSISTENCY throughout a task in the style or form of presentation (at own discretion in the absence of instructions) of the following:

    (a) abbreviations indicating measurements/weights/times/money

    (b) words/figures ie using words and/or figures systematically for quantities

    (c) words/symbols (including dash/hyphen key for 'to') eg % or per cent; May — June or May-June

    (d) punctuation (open or full style; spacing system)

    (e) paragraphing including numbered/lettered paragraphs, sub-paragraphs and listed items (indented or blocked; spacing system)

    (f) alternative spelling

    (g) line-spacing within and between paragraphs, listed items

    (h) leader dots

    (i) material in columns

C.4 INSET indicated portions of a task as instructed, from left-hand margins

C.5 USE capitals, spaced capitals, initial capitals with underlining, for emphasis in headings and in text, as shown in draft

C.6 (a) CENTRE lines as instructed

    (b) in the absence of specific instructions USE CONSISTENTLY blocked or centred style at own discretion for same type of item throughout a task, eg paragraphs in one style with headings in another is not a fault

C.7 USE specified line-spacing

C.8 ALLOCATE SPACE of specified size (which may be expressed in terms of measurement or line-spacing), eg for margins, addresses, illustrations, letterheads

C.9 (a) ADJUST line length as instructed

    (b) In the absence of instructions ENSURE an aggregate of right and left-hand margins of at least 25 mm (1 in), and aggregate of top and bottom margins of at least 25 mm (1 in)

C.10 LEAVE, in the absence of instructions, a minimum of one clear line-space

    (a) before and after headings

    (b) between complimentary close and signatory

    (c) before/after separate items within a document, eg date, reference

C.11 USE justified/ragged right margin as instructed

4 **Form of Assessment**

4.1   Candidates will be assessed in a 1½ hour production test set and marked by RSA and
consisting of 4 practical single-page word processing tasks which are related to a
single organisation.

4.2   Nature of tasks: the material given will be:

(a)   such as is likely to be routinely and ordinarily given to a beginner word process
operator in an office

(b)   concerned with topics drawn from the business functions common to the majority
of business, commerce and professional offices; eg purchasing, personnel,
accounts.

4.3   The stationery provided for completion of the tasks will be:

A4 plain white — 6 sheets.
No additional stationery will be allowed.

Candidates using machines which will not take the stationery provided may use equal
amounts of stationery provided by the centre; **a note by the Invigilator must be
returned with the worked scripts.** If continuous stationery is used, the pages should
be separated before insertion in the candidate's folder.

4.4   Instructions not under Objective B.3 will be given in handwriting and circled to
distinguish them from the text

4.5   Candidates may use calculators, English and mother-tongue dictionaries, spellcheckers, and centre-prepared or manufacturers' manuals in the examination.
RSA does not provide these and candidates are advised to check with their centres well
before the examination whether they need to bring any of them

4.6   The printing may be carried out by the tutor or other person appointed by the local
secretary.

4.7   The printing may be done outside the 1½ hours allowed for the examination.

4.8   *All* printing must be closely supervised and those involved must be instructed that,
after the examination time, NO CHANGES WHATSOEVER MAY BE MADE TO THE
DOCUMENTS PREPARED OTHER THAN LINES OF RULING AND INSERTION OF
CHARACTERS NOT AVAILABLE ON THE KEYBOARD OR PRINTER.

5 **Criteria of Assessment**

Marking Scheme

Obvious machine faults will not be penalised.

A PRODUCTION RATE

All tasks to be completed (except for omissions at the end of tasks which may be counted within tolerances for Section B, see paragraph 6).

Candidates' work will not be marked under Sections B and C unless all the tasks have been submitted.

B ACCURACY OF CONTENT

An Accuracy fault is ascribed to any word which is not 100% accurate when compared with given test material.

A word is defined as

(a)   any normally recognisable word (hyphenated words count as one)
(b)   any series of characters (including spaces where appropriate) which constitute a recognisable unit, eg postcode, initials or group of initials, courtesy title, line of dots, line of ruling, numbers, simple or compound measurements
(c)   including following or associated punctuation and spacing.

One Accuracy fault only will be ascribed to any one word (eg "acom-odatoin" counts only as one Accuracy fault in spite of several faults in the word) but Presentation faults may be applied in addition.

The same fault appearing more than once counts as an Accuracy fault each time.

There are 3 main types of Accuracy fault:

1 *Keying/spelling/punctuation faults:*
   These are words which:

1.1   contain a character, which is incorrect or illegible for any reason
1.2   have omitted or additional characters or spaces within the word
1.3   have no space following them
      have more than 2 spaces following them, except where appropriate, eg
      in spaced capitals, before postcode, in work with justified margins

      (Symbols and figures (eg £10), measurements eg 3' 6") etc count as one word
      (see (b) above) and may include space(s) if used systematically - see C.3.)

1.4   do not contain initial capitals in essential instances ie for proper nouns and at
      the beginning of sentences, or contain grammatically incorrect initial capitals.
      (Failure to insert a capital following a penalty for an omitted full stop will not be
      penalised.)

2 *Omissions and additions:*

One Accuracy fault will be ascribed to:

2.1 each word which is:
— the wrong word (replacing a word)
— omitted (and not replaced)
— added (not replacing a word)
— not removed as instructed

2.2 omission of *implied* instructions - penalties will be limited to the minimum number of words essential to fulfil the objective
— for failure to indicate an enclosure

2.3 each instance of failure to indicate paragraph as per draft.

3 Transpositions and misplacements:

One Accuracy fault will be ascribed to each instance of words:

— not transposed in accordance with an amendment to text under Objective B.3
— inserted in wrong order or place, eg misplaced within text or as foot or marginal note, regardless of the amount of material involved (in addition to any Accuracy faults which may be incurred under B.1 above).

C PRESENTATION OF WORK

One Presentation fault will be recorded for each:

C.1 task on incorrect stationery — *except* when centre has notified use of own stationery
C.2 instance of work which does not fit onto an A4 page
C.3 inconsistency in items (a) to (i) — ONE penalty only throughout a task for each item:

(a) abbreviations indicating measurements/weights/ times/money
(b) words/figures used randomly for quantities
(c) words/symbols (including dash/hyphen key for 'to') — word and symbol used; inconsistent spacing
(d) punctuation (at least one space required after punctuation mark) (NB if no space, Accuracy fault — see B.1.4)
(e) paragraphing including numbered/lettered paragraphs, sub-paragraphs and listed items — indented and blocked used randomly; horizontal spacing inconsistent
(f) alternative spellings
(g) line-spacing within and between paragraphs, listed items
(h) leader dots
(i) material in columns (ie blocked/indented/centred) — whole *figures* may be ranged to the left or the right of a column; *words* may be ranged to the left, blocked or centred

C.4   indicated portions of a task not inset from left-hand margin as instructed

C.5   instance of capitals/spaced capitals/initial capitals with underlining for emphasis in
headings and in text not as shown in draft

(Unrequested underlining or emboldening of headings will not be penalised.
Consistent incorrect use of capitals and/or underlining in related headings within a
task will incur 1 penalty only.)

C.6   (a)   line not centred as instructed
(b)   task in which blocked or centred style (at own discretion) not used consistently
for the same type of item throughout a task (eg paragraphs in one style with
headings in another style is not a fault). Centred style headings and/or material
in notices/advertisements not technically accurate to within 13 mm (0.5 in)
horizontally. (NB 1 fault only if all examples are consistent with a major item
centred inaccurately.)

C.7   instance of failure to comply with an instruction about line-spacing

C.8   allocation of space

(a)   as specified in line-spaces not accurate
(b)   as specified in measurements not *at least* given size

C.9   (a)   line length not as instructed
(b)   aggregate of right and left margins of at least 25 mm (1 in); and an aggregate of
top and bottom margins of at least 25 mm (1 in)

task with irregular left margin not attributable to machine fault, nor to intentional
variance for sub-paragraphs, listed items, etc.

C.10   instance of *no* clear line-space, in the absence of instructions, at points (a) to (c) —
ONE penalty only throughout a task for each item:

(a)   before and after headings
(b)   for signature on letters
(c)   before and after separate items within a document

C.11   instance of regular justified/ragged right margins not produced as instructed.

6 Certification

6.1   Results will be graded Distinction, Pass or Fail.

6.2   For award of a **Stage I Certificate with Distinction** candidates must fulfil:

Objective A by working at a Production Rate of 300 words per hour (ie completing all
the 4 tasks)
Objective B with no more than 2 Accuracy faults
and
Objective C with no more than 2 Presentation faults.

6.3   For award of a **Stage I Pass Certificate** candidates must fulfil:

Objective A by working at a Production Rate of 300 words per hour (ie completing all the 4 tasks)
Objective B with no more than 7 Accuracy faults
and
Objective C with no more than 5 Presentation faults

6.4   The result slips issued to all candidates will indicate the grade awarded for Objectives A, B and C.

Section 4:
Exam Practice

Preparing for your exam

In the exam you will have to complete 4 tasks in 1½ hours. Three of the tasks will be recalled documents (previously keyed in for you) and one task you will have to key in yourself.

As it is not possible to supply you with the 3 recalled documents on disk, you will have to key them in yourself, following the instructions provided.

Make sure you study the notes for candidates on page 98, and take care to follow the handwritten instructions at the beginning of each task. As you will be using the 3 recalled documents for each exam paper, it is important that you save each task under the name given and NOT under the original name, ie recall **Task 1,** complete it, and then save as **T11192** (this name represents the Task number, the month and year of the exam paper). By following this procedure you will be able to use the original keyed-in documents for each of the exam papers included in this book.

Good luck with the practice papers on the following pages. The practice routine below will help you achieve success in your exam.

```
Exam practice routine:

Read and follow all instructions
Key in/edit within time limit
Use spellcheck
Proof-read screen copy and edit if necessary
View then print document
Proof-read print-out and edit if necessary
Save document
Repeat procedure for each exam task
On completion, check with answers
In class, hand in for marking
```

Exam documents

The following documents are required for the practice exam papers on pages 99 to 110. Key them in now, following the instructions provided.

Task 1

Key in the document below, using either a justified or a ragged right margin. Save but DO NOT PRINT. Name your document **TASK 1**.

```
Ref SC/KMB

Dear Sirs

Thank you for your recent letter.   We give below the details
you require:

Please do not hesitate to contact this office if you require
any further information.

We look forward to hearing from you again in the future.

Yours faithfully
PRAXITELES GROUP



Gilbert Lay
General Manager
```

Tasks 1, 2 and 4 are the master documents for your exam papers. Please proof-read them carefully before you save them.

Task 2
Key in the following document in single line spacing with a ragged right margin. Save but DO NOT PRINT. Name your document **TASK 2.**

From the moment you start earning you should think about insurance. You can begin with very simple life assurance. This is a good way to start saving.

As your circumstances change, your policy can be adapted to suit your needs. Payments can be made monthly and are often surprisingly small.

Task 4

Key in the following document with a ragged right margin and a line length of
65 characters or 16.5 cm (6.5 in). Save but DO NOT PRINT. Name your document
Task 4.

```
Bargains Galore

Praxiteles Superb Offers

We take great pleasure in inviting you to visit our showrooms to
view our superb offers.  Our sale starts at the beginning of next
month and will run for the rest of the month.
```

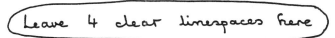

```
If you come along on the first day of our sale we are able to
offer you an extra discount.  This is in addition to the 10 per
cent available on most of our merchandise.

On Mondays and Tuesdays additional bargains will be available on
selected items.  Contact Mrs Anne Myers for details.

Come along and see for yourself.
```

RSA notes

The following instructions are reprinted from the RSA Stage I Word Processing exam papers.

RSA EXAMINATIONS BOARD

Notes for Candidates

1   Please include your name, centre number and Task number on every document, either at the top or bottom of the page.
2   English and mother-tongue dictionaries, spellcheckers, calendars, calculators and centre-prepared or manufacturers' manuals may be used during the examination.
3   The printing of the Tasks may be done outside the 1½ hours allowed, but no amendments can be made to the text after that time has expired, other than lines of ruling and insertion of characters not available on the keyboard or printer. Your Invigilator will tell you the exact instructions for your centre.

You must:

1   Complete all 4 Tasks
2   Use only the stationery provided in your answer book.*
3   Insert today's date on letters unless otherwise instructed.

Penalties will be incurred if these instructions are not followed.

---

* Candidates using machines which will not take the stationery provided may use equal amounts of stationery provided by the centre; a note by the Invigilator must be returned with the scripts. If continuous stationery is used, the pages should be separated before insertion in the candidate's folder.

A197 Word Processing Stage I (4-18 November 1992)

Time allowed: 1½ hours

Recall this letter stored under TASK 1 and address it to The Card Box Laurel Way BRADFORD BD16 8WX Please mark it URGENT and insert the following information where indicated. Save under T11192 and print one copy. You may use either a justified or ragged right margin.

PRINTED   CHRISTMAS   CARDS

Insert as a heading above the first paragraph

Tab Set
0.5"
2.25"
3.5"

DESIGN	SIZE	PRICE PER 100
Winter	6" square	£30.00
Christmas Carols	8" square	£37.00
The Shepherds	7" square	£34.50

Insert this table after paragraph which ends 'details you require.'

An example of our printed cards is attached and any orders must be received by the end of November to be sure they arrive before Christmas.

Add to end of the paragraph which ends 'any further information'.

A197 Word Processing Stage I (Contd)

Task
2

Recall the document stored under TASK 2 and key in the additional information as indicated. Also correct the errors circled. Save under T2 1192 and print one copy. A justified or ragged right margin may be used.

There is always many new things you want to buy when you first begin work. It is very important not to wast your money Spend some time and thought planing your budget carefully. There are plenty of poeple waiting to advise you and give you help.

From the moment you start earning you should think about insurance. You can begin with very simple life assurance. This is a good way to start saving.

As your circumstances change, your policy can be adapted to suit your needs.

When you move out of rented accomodation into your own house you should insure it. You can also take out a policy to cover the house content's and your belongings against theft or damage.

Payments can be made monthly and are often surprisingly small.

A197 Word Processing Stage I (Contd)

Please key in the details below in single linespacing and save under T 31192. Print one copy. Choose either ragged or justified right margin.

inset 10 character spaces or 25 mm (1") from left margin.

HOMES   DESIGN AWARDS

We are pleased to announce the winners of the local Homes Design Awards. This yr. there are awards for estate design and best house.

The Gold Medal for estate design goes to Praxi Homes for their new housing development in Pinewood Dr., Little Oakton.

The houses have been designed to blend in w. existing buildings. They are built around a private drive leading off the main thro' road. The gardens are planted with a ~~variety~~ range of trees and shrubs. Our judges thought the layout overall gave an open look to the estate. They were impressed, too, by the ~~number of~~ wooded areas which have been retained ~~trees left to grow.~~

use double linespacing for this paragraph

The same co. also wins the Best House Award for one of their family houses. They build several styles, ~~ranging from small detached cottages to the large executive homes,~~ all of wh. are well designed. Our award, however, goes to the Wessex, for its outstanding design and value

The house has 4 bedrooms, ~~all of which have mirrored wardrobes.~~ with fitted wardrobes in each There is a large lounge and sep. dining room with French windows. The kitchen is well planned with plenty of oak units and cupboards. ~~The master bedroom is big and has an en suite shower room.~~ There are very good quality fittings and careful attention has been given to detail throughout.

The judges think that this house will def. become very popular. We ack. with thanks the help we have recd. in making these awards. A presentation wl. be made to Praxi Homes next Fri. at 2 pm.

A197 Word Processing Stage I (Contd)

Recall this document stored under TASK 4
Amend where shown and save under T41192. Adjust
margins to give a line length of 45 characters or 11.5cm (4½").
Print one copy with a justified right margin.

Bargains Galore ← **Spaced Caps**

Praxiteles Superb Offers ← **Centre**

We take great pleasure in inviting you to visit our showrooms to
view our ~~superb offers~~. [toys] Our sale starts at the beginning of next
month and will run for the rest of the month.

Praxiteles Bargain Basement is moving premises. All
stock must go.
Leave only 1 linespace here **Change to Caps**

If you come along on the first day of our sale we are able to
offer you ~~an extra discount. This is in addition to the~~ 10 per
cent ~~available on most~~ of our merchandise. [discount on the majority]

~~On Mondays and Tuesdays additional bargains will be available on
selected items.~~ Contact Mrs Anne Myers for details.

Come along and see for yourself.

We have dolls' prams in various sizes. The smallest will
suit children aged 2. We have dolls that can walk
and talk. Our train sets come with large amounts
of track. You can cover an attic floor if you wish!

We have a large selection of simple reading
books. Many are educational.
Leave 4 clear linespaces here

Please come along to Praxiteles B—— B——
situated at Kirby Street, Bradford.

Hope you managed to complete all the tasks for the November 1992 Paper. From now on, allow yourself approximately 15-20 minutes per task, so that you have time to proof-read carefully.

N197 Word Processing Stage I (18-27 January 1993)

Time allowed: 1½ hours

Recall this letter stored under TASK1
and address it to E R Crabb Ltd
19 Abbey Court STOCKPORT SK19 3JX
Please mark it URGENT and insert the
following information where indicated.
Save under TI193 and print one copy.
You may use either a justified or
ragged right margin.

BUSINESS EQUIPMENT EXHIBITIONS

Insert as a heading above the first paragraph

DATE	VENUE	TOWN/CITY
2 June	Kingston Hall	Manchester
10 July	Edinburgh Hotel	Leeds
12 June	Regent Hall	Blackburn

Insert this table as the second paragraph

We were very sorry you could not attend
the recent exhibition but hope to see
you at one of the events shown on
the enclosed brochure.

Insert this paragraph before the final paragraph.

N197 Word Processing Stage I (Contd)

> Recall the document stored under TASK 2
> and key in the additional information as
> indicated. Also correct the errors circled.
> Save under   T2193   and print one copy.
> A justified or ragged right margin may be used.

From the moment you start earning you should think about insurance. You can begin with very simple life assurance. This is a good way to start saving.

Many policies allow you to have the money plus a good bonus after a certain number of years. Should you die before then your dependants will receive it. If anything (hapens) to you your (famliy) will be taken care of. It is very comforting to know this.

As your circumstances change, your policy can be adapted to suit your needs. Payments can be made monthly and are often surprisingly small.

When you find your house (have) been burgled it is very upsetting. (however it is easier to cope if you are well (insurred.) With the (companys) help you can replace your (stollen) belongings.

N197 Word Processing Stage I (Contd)

> Please key in the details below in single linespacing and save under T·3193. Print one copy. Choose either ragged or justified right margin.

MOVE TO NEW OFFICES

You are all aware that next month the co. will be relocating to the new Weston Rd. site.

The factory and warehouse /accom. is not yet ready. There have been problems w. the supply of fittings. These have been now resolved and it is hoped that the delay in completion will not be too long.

[Use double linespacing for this paragraph]
The office staff will move as ~~arranged~~ planned. This will not be an easy task. We bel. however that we shd. be able to achieve it quickly and efficiently with yr. help and co-operation.

[Inset 5 character spaces or 13mm (½") from left margin]
The Finance Office will be the first to move ~~move before the other offices~~. This will require a shut-down of all computer systems from Thursday night until Sun. evening. All computer personnel are asked to work over the weekend to ensure a smooth changeover. You will rec. extra payment for this work. // All other offices wl. move on Saturday. Key personnel ~~and those who have already been asked by their managers~~ must attend during this time. Staff ~~will be able to claim days~~ may take time off in lieu by arrangement with their department head.

Customers will be advised of the move and asked not to make any a/c. enquiries during that week. All other bus. will progress as normal. ~~It is not a reason for a delay in services~~

Internal telephones may not be fully working for the first few days. Until they are, office juniors will act as messengers between offices. If any problems arise please inform the Office Manager.

> Please keep messages to a minimum.

N197 Word Processing Stage I (Contd)

> Recall this document stored under TASK 4.
> Amend where shown and save under T4193.
> Adjust margins to give a line length of 50 characters, or
> 12.5 cm (5"). Print one copy with justified right margin.

Bargains Galore ← (Spaced Caps)

Praxiteles Superb Offers ← (Caps)

~~We take great pleasure in inviting you to visit our showrooms to view our superb offers.~~ Our sale starts at the beginning of next month and will run for the rest of the month.

We at Praxiteles Office Furniture would like ~~to invite~~ you to a Special Preview.

(Leave only 3 linespaces here)

If you come along on the first day of our sale we ~~are able to~~ can offer you an extra discount. This is in addition to the 10 per cent available on most of our merchandise.

~~On Mondays and Tuesdays additional bargains will be available on selected items.~~ Contact Mrs Anne Myers ~~for details~~ as soon as possible.

(Leave 2 clear linespaces here)

Praxiteles O —— F —— has the latest in executive desks. These are made of teak or mahogany. We have luxury swivel chairs in grey, black or brown. You can choose from a wide range of desks and chairs for your typists. Some of our new desks include space for your computer, printer and stationery. We have 4-drawer filing cabinets which lock.

Come along and see for yourself. ← (Centre this line)

Well done!
Exam papers get
easier the more
you do.

E197 Word Processing Stage I (1-16 March 1993)

Time allowed: 1½ hours

Recall this letter stored under   TASK 1
and address it to J Johnson Ltd
Evelyn Road LIVERPOOL L68 9DE
Please mark it URGENT and insert the
following information where indicated.
Save under T1393   and print one copy.
You may use either a justified or ragged
right margin.

HEALTH   AND   SAFETY   AT   WORK

Insert as a heading after 'Dear Sirs'

SUBJECT	POSTER NO	SIZE
The electronic office	XRX439	A2
Know your escape route	PXT551	A1
Protect your building	SAC692	A3

Insert this table after the first paragraph

We have all the above posters in stock
at present and enclose a list of our
leaflets which may be helpful to you.

Add to end of the paragraph which ends 'any further information'.

E197 Word Processing Stage I (Contd)

Recall the document stored under TASK 2 and key in the additional information as indicated. Also correct the errors circled. A justified or ragged right margin may be used. Save as T2393 and print one copy.

From the moment you start earning you should think about insurance. Our sales staff are on hand to offer advice. An (agents) number is always given. Please feel free to ring him at any time.

You can begin with very simple life assurance. This is a good way to start saving. After a (miminum) number of years you can cash in the policy. (Hopefuly) a large bonus will have been added to your initial investment which can be useful if you are buying a new car or even a house. (Annother) type of insurance (take) care of these items.

As your circumstances change, your policy can be adapted to suit your needs. Payments can be made monthly and are often surprisingly small. (You will find (insureance) is a worthwhile expenditure.

E197 Word Processing Stage I (Contd)

Please key in the details below in single linespacing and save under T3393. Print one copy. Choose either ragged or justified right margin.

Inset this paragraph 10 character spaces or 25mm (1") from left margin.

QUARTERLY SALES REVIEW

This last quarter has seen a rise in demand for our products. ~~We have been very pleased with sales in all regions.~~ Thanks are due to the splendid effort put in by all our sales staff.

Early in the year we ~~published~~ produced a sales cat. for the first time. This has helped to promote a wide interest in our products.

The stained glass windows wh. were introduced last yr. are very popular. Our designers have started work on a new range with a Victorian theme.

We recom. making this a sales feature as soon as it is ready. In the meantime, we must maintain our efforts to increase sales of current designs ~~sell more of our other styles~~.

The French windows w. leaded lights are selling well. They have been bought mainly by hotels. We shd. now try to encourage other customers to invest in these.

This paragraph in double linespacing

We have recd. many enquiries in response to our adverts for etched mirrors. Unfortunately there is a temp. delay in making these. We sh. be writing to customers to explain the problem. It is hoped production will begin soon.

Last month we won a major contract for a new shopping arcade in Dudley. This includes internal and external windows and doors to shop units. ~~Mirrored tiles and glass dividers are also part of the contract.~~ The work wl. last for 12 months. // Sales are (overall/increasing) despite the poor bus. climate. We feel confident sales will continue to grow steadily in the future ~~expand over the next few years~~.

Work will begin next week.

E197 Word Processing Stage I (Contd)

Recall this document stored under TASK 4.
Amend where shown and save under T4393. Adjust
margins to give a line length of 55 characters or 14 cm (5½").
Print one copy with a justified right margin.

Double Glazing Sale ← Spaced Caps
~~Bargains Galore~~

Praxiteles Superb Offers

We take great pleasure in <u>inviting you to visit our showrooms to</u>
<u>view our superb offers.</u> Our sale starts at the beginning of next
month and will run for the ~~rest of the~~ month.
whole

Leave only 1 linespace here

If you come along ~~on the first day of our sale~~ we are able to
offer you an extra discount. This is in addition to the 10 per
cent available on most of our merchandise.

~~On Mondays and Tuesdays additional bargains will be available on~~
~~selected items. Contact Mrs Anne Myers for details.~~

Come along and see for yourself. ← Centre and Caps
Leave 2 clear linespaces here
Praxiteles Double Glazing will keep your house much
warmer in the winter. It will keep the heat in,
exclude draughts and add value to
your house.

Praxiteles D —— G —— adds security to your
home, reduces noise and saves energy.

Our <u>Sealed Units</u> have the optimum space width
of 12 mm between the layers of glass.

An absorbing agent is placed between the layers
of glass to ensure the air stays moisture free. This
avoids condensation forming.

Well
done — good
luck with your
exam. Hope you've
enjoyed your
learning!

Section 5:
WordPerfect 5.1 Instructions

Key
* = Required for Stage I
No symbol = Extra functions, not required for exam

* Adjusting line length

This is an alternative way of asking you to set new margins. As the default for WordPerfect is 10 pitch which gives 82 characters per line, you take away the line length required from 82 to find the total for both margins. To adjust line length to 50:

1 Width of paper (82) minus line length required (50) = 32
2 Divide 32 between left and right margins (32 ÷ 2 = 16)
3 Press **SHIFT + F8** (format)
4 Select **1** (line) and **7** (margins left and right)
5 Type in new margins (16 and 16) and press **ENTER**
6 Press **F7**

* Allocating space

* Down the page
Six single lines of typescript measures 25 mm (1 in), so if you are asked to leave 1 in clear down the page, you should press **RETURN** 7 times so that you leave 6 clear lines and then type on the seventh.

* Across the page
If you are asked to leave a space across the page you must consider the pitch you are using. The most common ones are 12 pitch (12 characters = 25 mm/1 in) and 10 pitch (10 characters = 25 mm/1 in).

WordPerfect 5.1 usually prints in 10 pitch, so to leave a space of 1 in across the page you must set a tab 10 spaces in from the left margin.

* Blocking text

When you block text it becomes highlighted. You can then alter its appearance, move, copy or delete it.

* To block text
1 Position cursor at beginning of text to be blocked
2 Press **F12** or **ALT + F4**
3 Move cursor to end of text to be blocked — the text will highlight as you move cursor
4 The block is now ready to be amended.

* To copy a block of text
1 Mark block of text to be copied following steps 1-3 above
2 Press **CTRL + F4** and **1** (**1** = marked block)
3 Select action **2** (**1** = move, **2** = copy, **3** = delete)
4 Position cursor where you want text to be copied to
5 Press **ENTER**

* To delete a block of text

1   Mark block of text to be deleted following steps 1-3 in *To Block Text* above
2   Press **CTRL + F4** and **1** (**1** = marked block)
3   Select action **3** (**1** = move, **2** = copy, **3** = delete)

* To move a block of text

1   Mark block of text to be moved
2   Press **CTRL + F4** and **1** (**1** = marked block)
3   Select action **1** (**1** = move, **2** = copy, **3** = delete)
4   Position cursor where you want text to be moved to
5   Press **ENTER**

* Cancelling commands

F1 will cancel any command you have just entered.

* Centring text

* Horizontally

Press **SHIFT + F6** and then key in text.

To centre more than one line of text, eg a menu:

1   Press **SHIFT + F8** (format), select **1** (line), **3** (justification)
2   Select **2** (centre), press **F7** to return to document
3   Key in text to be centred
4   Repeat steps **1** and **2**
5   Select **1** (left justify) or **4** (full) as required

To centre text when editing, place cursor at beginning of line to be centred and press **SHIFT + F6** or, for a longer piece of text:

1   Position cursor on first character of text to be centred
2   Press **F12** or **ALT + F4** to switch block on
3   Move the cursor to end of text to be centred
4   Press **SHIFT + F6**

Vertically

1   Position cursor at top of page
2   Press **SHIFT + F8** (format)
3   Select **2** (page), **1** (centre page top to bottom)
4   Press **Y** (yes), press **F7** to return to document

Codes

In WordPerfect, codes determine how your text looks both on the screen and at the printer. However, these codes are not shown in the normal editing screen. Sometimes unwanted or misplaced codes can cause problems so it is useful to be able to reveal these codes when necessary.

To reveal codes

Press **F11** or **ALT + F3** to reveal codes (repeat to return to normal editing screen). This divides the screen into two parts. The top part is the normal editing screen while the lower part displays the same text, accompanied by the codes it contains.

To delete codes (normal screen)

1   Place cursor at beginning of text where code was inserted
2   Press backspace key (←) to delete code
3   Delete code **Y/N**? — press **Y**

To delete codes (reveal codes screen)

1   Press **ALT + F3** to reveal codes
2   Move cursor to code to be deleted and press **DEL** key
3   Press **ALT + F3** to return to normal editing screen

* Copying text (copy and paste)

1   Position cursor on first character of text to be copied
2   Press **CTRL + F4**, select text to be copied (**1** = sentence, **2** = paragraph, **3** = page)
3   Select action **2** (**1** = move, **2** = copy, **3** = delete)
4   Position cursor where you want text to be copied to
5   Press **ENTER**

Text to be copied can also be selected by 'highlighting' or 'blocking':

1   Position cursor on first character of text to be copied
2   Press **F12** or **ALT + F4** to switch block on
3   Move cursor to end of text to be copied
4   Press **CTRL + F4** and **1** (**1** = marked block). Continue with steps 3-5 above.

* Creating a document

Entering WordPerfect automatically creates a new document.

* Cursor control (moving about the screen)

←	one character left
→	one character right
↑	one line up
↓	one line down
CTRL ←	one word to the left
CTRL →	one word to the right
HOME ←	beginning of line
HOME →	end of line
END	end of line
HOME ↑	top of screen
HOME ↓	bottom of screen
HOME, HOME ↑	beginning of document
HOME, HOME ↓	end of document
PAGE UP	one page up
PAGE DOWN	one page down
CTRL, HOME (page)	go to page

* Deleting text

DEL	deletes at cursor position
BACKSPACE (←)	deletes text to left of cursor
CTRL BACKSPACE	deletes word at cursor position
CTRL END	deletes from cursor to end of line
CTRL PAGE DOWN	deletes from cursor to end of page

* To delete large areas of text

1   Position cursor on first character of text to be deleted
2   Press **CTRL + F4**, select text to be deleted (**1** = sentence, **2** = paragraph, **3** = page)
3   Select action **3** (**1** = move, **2** = copy, **3** = delete).

Text to be deleted can also be selected by 'blocking':

1   Press **F12** or **ALT + F4** and move cursor to block text
2   Press **DEL** key, **delete block?** — **Y** for Yes.

Deleting files

1   Press **F5** and type **a:** (list files on floppy disk), press **ENTER**
2   Position cursor on file to be deleted
3   Press **2** (delete), **Y** (to confirm)
4   Press **F7** to return to normal editing screen

* Emphasising text

($^$ = CTRL KEY)

bold	**F6** (before and after text)
underline	**F8** (before and after text)
italics	**^ + F8, 2, 4** (before and after text)
large print	**^ + F8, 1, 5** (before and after text)
very large print	**^ + F8, 1, 6** (before and after text)
extra large print	**^ + F8, 1, 7** (before and after text)
centre	**SHIFT + F6**
right align	**ALT + F6**
different fonts (pitch)	**^ + F8, 4**, select font required
	(then return to original font)

CLOSED CAPITALS

S P A C E D   C A P I T A L S

Initial Capitals

* To emphasise text after keying in

Text can also be emphasised after keying in by 'highlighting' or 'blocking':

1   At beginning of text press **F12** or **ALT + F4** to switch block on
2   Move cursor to end of text to be emphasised
3   Press emphasis code required (**F6** = bold, **F8** = underline, **^ + F8, 2, 4** = italics, **^ + F8 , 1, 5** = large print)

NB To centre and right align after keying in, position cursor at beginning of text and press **SHIFT + F6** or **ALT + F6**.

* To alter capitalisation after keying in

Text can be changed from lower case to upper case (and vice versa) after keying in.

1   At beginning of text to be changed press **F12** or **ALT + F4** to switch block on
2   Move cursor to end of text to be changed
3   Press **SHIFT + F3** and select **1** (upper case) or **2** (lower case)

To delete emphasis codes

1   Position cursor at beginning of text and press **Backspace** key
2   Press **Y** to delete code.

OR

1   Reveal codes (**ALT + F3**)
2   Position cursor on code to be deleted and press **DEL**
3   **ALT + F3** to return to normal editing screen

* Floppy disks

New disks are completely blank and must be formatted before they can be used. The format program marks out the disk for storing data with electronic markings by dividing it into tracks and sectors.

To format a disk
1   Exit from WordPerfect to **C:\\>**
2   Type **Format A**: to format a disk in drive A
3   Insert disk into disk drive and press **ENTER**
4   When formatting process is complete, you will then be asked if you want to format another disk. Type **Y** if you do and follow the procedure or **N** to return to the **C:\\>**.

To label a disk
Write on the label before putting it on the disk — you may damage your disk if you use a biro. If you have to write on the label when it is on the disk, use a felt tip pen.

To take a back-up copy of a floppy disk
You should regularly copy all your disks in case the originals get damaged.

1   Make sure you are in **Drive C** — prompt is **C:\\ >**
2   Type **diskcopy a: b:** and press **ENTER**
3   Insert source disk into drive and press **ENTER**
4   When prompted, remove source disk and insert destination disk into drive and press **ENTER**

Protecting a floppy disk
To protect your disks against being deleted, amended or edited, move the write-protect tab over the notch in a 3 ½ in disk or stick on a write-protect tab on a 5¼ in disk. Remove the write-protect tab to use the disk again.

* Fonts see Pitch

You can change the style of text you are using. This depends on the printer and the way your machine has been set up.

* Function keys

		SHIFT +	ALT +	CTRL +
F1	cancel	set up	thesaurus	shell
F2	search →	search ←	replace	spell
F3	help	switch	reveal codes	screen
F4	→ indent	→ indent ←	block	move
F5	list files	date/outline	mark text	text in/out
F6	bold	centre	flush right	tab align
F7	exit	print	columns/tables	footnote
F8	underline	format	style	font
F9	merge	merge codes	graphics	merge/sort
F10	save	retrieve	macro	macro define
F11	reveal codes			
F12	block			

117

* Hard space see Line endings

* Help menu

1   Press **F3**
2   Type initial letter of whatever you need help with
3   Screen will show features that start with the initial letter you selected and where the feature is found
4   For function keys press **F3** and then the function key
5   Press **ENTER** to return to your document

* Housekeeping

This is the general routine of organising your documents and disks, etc. It covers deleting, copying and renaming documents.

To carry out any of the following activities press **F5** and type **a:**. Press **ENTER** to list the files on your disk.

Deleting a document
1   Move cursor to document you wish to delete
2   Select **2** (delete)
3   Type **Y** and the document will be deleted

Renaming a document
1   Move cursor to document you wish to rename
2   Select **3** (rename)
3   Type new name and press **ENTER**

Copying a document
1   Move cursor to document you wish to copy
2   Select **8** (copy)
3   Type new document name and press **ENTER**
4   Select **7** and press **ENTER** twice — document will appear in list of files

Hyphenation

The appearance of your document can be improved by dividing words at the end of a line.

To switch on hyphenation
1   At beginning of document press **SHIFT + F8**
2   Select **1** (line) and **1** (hyphenation)
3   Press **Y** (yes) to switch on, **F7** to return to document
4   As you move down your document, it will be reformatted

To switch off hyphenation

1   At beginning of document press **SHIFT + F8**
2   Select **1** (line) and **1** (hyphenation)
3   Press **N** (no) to switch off, **F7** to return to document
4   Delete first hyphen in each paragraph
5   As you move through your document, it will be reformatted

* Hard hyphen

To prevent hyphenated words splitting at the end of a line, eg *Ross-Jones*, you can use a hard hyphen. When you are keying in, if you notice that you are near the end of a line:

1   Type first word, eg *Ross*
2   Press **HOME HYPHEN**
3   Type next word, eg *Jones*
4   *Ross* and *Jones* will have a hyphen between but will be kept together

When you are proof-reading your document, if you notice that hyphenated words have been split:

1   Position cursor on hyphen between words
2   Delete hyphen — words will be joined together
3   Press **HOME HYPHEN** to insert a hard hyphen between them.

* Inserting/overtyping

You are usually in insert mode. Position cursor where you want to insert text and key in. Press **INS** key to change to typeover mode; text keyed in will overtype (and delete) existing text. Press **INS** to return to insert mode.

Insetting/indenting see **Paragraphs**

* Justifying text

Text is automatically fully justified. To switch off justification you should select left justify only.

1   Place cursor at beginning of your document
2   Press **SHIFT + F8, 1, 3, 1** (left justify only), **F7**

To switch on justification, press **SHIFT + F8, 1, 3, 4** (full justification) or reveal codes (**F11** or **ALT + F3**) and delete **JUST LEFT** code.

* Line endings

To prevent words splitting at end of line, eg *Mr Smith*, you can use a hard space. When you are keying in, if you notice that you are near the end of a line:

1 Type first word, eg *Mr*
2 Press **HOME** key then space bar
3 Type next word, eg *Smith*
4 *Mr Smith* will be kept together

When you are proof-reading your document, if you notice that words have been split:

1 Position cursor on space between words
2 Delete space — words will be joined together
3 Press **HOME** key then space bar to insert a hard space between them.

(See **Hyphenation** for hard hyphens at line ends.)

* Line spacing

The default is set at single line spacing.

* Changing line spacing
1 Press **SHIFT + F8** (format)
2 Select **1** (line) and **6** (line spacing)
3 Type **2** for double line spacing and press **ENTER**
4 Press **F7** to return to document

* Listing files

Press **F5** to show the default directory at bottom of screen. Type **a:** and press **ENTER** to list the files on your floppy disk.

With your list of files on screen, you can retrieve, delete, rename, print or copy a file.

* Margins

The default for all margins is 25 mm (1 in). Left and right margins may be shown as 25 mm (1 in) or 10 (ie 10 characters).

Top and bottom margins are shown as 6 (6 lines = 25 mm/1 in).

* To change left and right margins
1 Press **SHIFT + F8** (format)
2 Select **1** (line) and **7** (margins left and right)
3 Type in new margins and press **ENTER**
4 Press **F7** to return to document

To change top and bottom margins
1   Press **SHIFT + F8** (format)
2   Select **2** (page) and **5** (margins top and bottom)
3   Type in new margins and press **ENTER**
4   Press **F7** to return to document

If you are using headed paper, measure the top and left/right margins required and set your margins accordingly.

* Moving text (cut and paste)

1   Position cursor on first character of text to be moved
2   Press **CTRL + F4**, select text to be moved (**1** = sentence, **2** = paragraph, **3** = page)
3   Select action **1** (**1** = move, **2** = copy, **3** = delete)
4   Position cursor where you want text to be moved to
5   Press **ENTER**

Text to be moved can also be selected by 'highlighting' or 'blocking' the text:

1   Position cursor on first character of text to be moved
2   Press **F12** or **ALT + F4** to switch block on
3   Move cursor to end of text to be moved
4   Press **CTRL + F4** and **1** (**1** = marked block). Continue with steps 3-5 above.

* Paragraphs (indenting/insetting/numbering)

* Indenting from left margin (first line of paragraph only)
1   Set tab stop at required position (**SHIFT + F8, 1, 8**)
2   Press **TAB** to indent first line only of paragraph

* Insetting from left margin (whole paragraph)
1   Set tab stop at required position (**SHIFT + F8, 1, 8**)
2   Press **F4** to inset whole paragraph
3   Press **ENTER** at end of paragraph to return to original margin

* Insetting from both margins (whole paragraph)
1   Set tab stop at required position (left only)
2   Press **SHIFT + F4** to inset whole paragraph by same amount from both margins
3   Press **ENTER** at end of paragraph to return to original margins

Numbering paragraphs
1   Set tab stop at required position (**SHIFT + F8, 1, 8**)
2   Key in number of paragraph
3   Press **F4** to inset whole paragraph OR press **TAB** to indent first line only

Set two tab stops if the number has to be inset from the margin.

* Pitch

The default pitch is set at 10 (10 characters per 25 mm/1 in). To change pitch:

1   Press **SHIFT + F8** (format), **3** (document)
2   Select **3** (initial base font)
3   Select pitch required and whole document will be changed to that pitch
4   Press **F7** to return to document

To change font for selected parts of your document:

1   Press **CTRL + F8**, **4** (base font)
2   Select font required
3   To return to original font press **CTRL + F8**, **4**
4   Select original font

* Printing

Make sure printer is set up and your station is selected.

* Printing from a document on screen
1   Press **SHIFT + F7** (print)
2   Select **1** (full document) or **2** (page)
3   To print certain pages select **5** (multiple pages)
4   Type in page numbers required and press **ENTER**

* Printing from disk
1   Press **SHIFT + F7** (print)
2   Select **3** (document on disk)
3   Type in document name and press **ENTER**
4   Press **ENTER** for **All** or select page numbers required and press **ENTER**

* Printing from list of files
1   Press **F5** and type **a:** (list files on floppy disk), press **ENTER**
2   Move cursor to highlight document
3   Select **4** (print)
4   Press **ENTER** for **All** or select page numbers required and press **ENTER**
5   Press **F7** to exit from list files

* Abandoning printing
1   Press **SHIFT + F7**, **4** (control printer)
2   Select **1** (cancel) and press **ENTER**
3   Press **F7** to exit from print screen

* Retrieving a document

1   At **list files** (**F5 a:**) highlight document to be retrieved
2   Press **1** to retrieve

OR

1   Press **SHIFT + F10** (retrieve)
2   Key in **a:(docname)** and press **ENTER**

* Reforming text

If your line breaks as you edit text it will automatically reformat when you move the cursor.

* Saving a document

All work should be saved on your floppy disk. If your machine does not default to drive **A**, always remember to type **A:docname**.

* Saving and clearing screen
1   Press **F7** (save document?), type **Y** (document name?), type in name under which you wish to store document
2   Press **ENTER** (exit WordPerfect?), type **N** to clear the screen, **F1** to continue editing the document, or **Y** to leave WordPerfect

* Saving but keeping document on screen
1   Press **F10** (document to be saved?), type in name under which you wish to store document
2   Press **ENTER**

When saving a document retrieved from disk, original name will appear. Press **ENTER** to save. Type **Y** if you wish to overwrite old version, or **N** and type in a new filename.

* Spellcheck

1   Position cursor on word or page to be checked or anywhere for full document
2   Press **CTRL + F2** (spell) and select either **1** (word), **2** (page) or **3** (document)
3   Cursor moves to any word mis-spelt and gives alternatives
4   Correct by typing letter next to suggested word. If correct word is not given, select **4** (edit) and make correction yourself, press **F7** to continue
5   If cursor stops at proper noun (ie a person's name or a place) or a correct word which WordPerfect does not recognise, select **2** (skip)
6   To stop spellcheck part way through, press **F1**
7   When spellcheck is complete, the number of words in document is given and a message tells you to press any key to continue.

* Status line

In WordPerfect your screen is usually blank except for the status line at bottom right which should show:

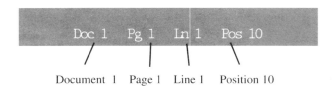

Doc 1   Pg 1   Ln 1   Pos 10

Document 1   Page 1   Line 1   Position 10

As the status line indicates position of cursor it will change as you key in your document.

* Subscripts and superscripts

* Subscripts
1   Press **CTRL + F8** (font), select **1** (size) and **2** (subscript)
2   Type text
3   Press **CTRL + F8**, **3** (normal) to switch off

* Superscripts
1   Press **CTRL + F8** (font), select **1** (size) and **1** (superscript)
2   Type text
3   Press **CTRL + F8**, **3** (normal) to switch off

* Switching off/exiting WordPerfect

1   Press **F7** (exit)
2   Save your work (if necessary)
3   Press **Y** to exit WordPerfect
4   At **C:/** or opening screen remove disk from drive
5   Carefully place disk in disk case
6   Select **PARK HARD DISK** from menu or, if at **C:/** , type **PARK** and press **ENTER**
7   Switch off machine

* Switching on/loading WordPerfect

1   Check equipment and switch on
2   When the operating system has loaded, insert your work disk into the floppy disk drive
3   Load WordPerfect. This will depend on how your machine has been set up. Consult your tutor/supervisor or your machine manual if necessary.

* Tabs

Tab stops are pre-set every 13 mm (0.5 in). To change them:

1   Press **SHIFT + F8** (format), **1** (line), **8** (tab set)
2   Clear existing tabs — **CTRL END**
3   Tap your space bar or cursor to position tabs
4   Press **L** for left, **C** for centre, **R** for right tab or **D** for decimal tab
5   Press **F7** twice to return to document

* Tabulation

In Stage I you will have a simple tab to insert in one of your documents. Use tab settings to align the columns and remember to leave equal space between columns.

Undeleting text

If you delete any text by mistake, press **F1** to 'undelete'. WordPerfect stores your last three deletions which you can display on screen and restore if necessary:

1   Press **F1**, last deletion will appear
2   Press **1** (restore) or **2** (previous deletion)
3   If you select **2** (previous deletion), you can scroll back through the deletions by pressing ↑ cursor key
4   When deletion required is highlighted, press **1** (restore) or **F1** to cancel

* Viewing before printing

Press **SHIFT + F7** (print), **6** (view document) to see what document will look like when printed. Press **F7** to return to normal screen.

* Wordwrap

DO NOT press **ENTER** or **RETURN** at end of a line. The text will automatically wrap to next line. Only press **ENTER** at end of a paragraph or after a heading (or other short line).

Index